Puzzle #1

6x6 Sudoku

	6	1	5		4
4		5			6
5			2	6	
2	1			5	
6	5	4		1	
1			6	4	

Puzzle #2

6x6 Sudoku

6			1		
		2	3	4	
5				6	
3	6				1
4	3		5	1	
	1		6		4

Puzzle #3

6x6 Sudoku

	5	3	1	2	6
	6	2			3
3	1		2		
		6			
6				5	2
		4	6	3	

Puzzle #4

6x6 Sudoku

5	4	3		1	
1		6	3		5
	3	5	4	6	1
3	1	4		5	
		2	1		4

Puzzle #5

6x6 Sudoku

2		5		3	6
	1		2	5	4
					2
	2	3		4	1
	6	2		1	3
1	3	4	6		

Puzzle #6

6x6 Sudoku

					1
3		4	2		
	6	3	5		4
4	5	1	3		6
6		2	1	5	
1	3	5		4	

Puzzle #7

6x6 Sudoku

2	5				4
6			1		
	6		2	5	
5		2	4	6	3
4	2	5		1	
		6		4	

Puzzle #8

6x6 Sudoku

4	5				
3			5	4	2
5			2	6	1
1					
2		5	4	3	6
6			1		5

Puzzle #9

6x6 Sudoku

	1			4	3
3					6
2	5			3	
6	3	1			
1		3	4		5
	6	5			2

Puzzle #10

6x6 Sudoku

1	4	6			2
3	2		1	6	
4		2	6	5	3
5	6			4	
2		4			

Puzzle #11

6x6 Sudoku

			6		
4	6			5	3
1	2	3			
				3	1
2	5			1	4
3	1	4	5		6

Puzzle #12

6x6 Sudoku

5	1		2		6
2	6	3	4	1	5
		6		2	
		2		6	1
	3	1		5	2
		5	1		

Puzzle #13

6x6 Sudoku

	3				6
5		1	3		
4	1	5		2	3
		3	4		5
	4	2	5	6	1
		6	2	3	

Puzzle #14

6x6 Sudoku

	2			1	
1	3			2	6
3	5	4		6	2
2	6	1	3		
5	1			3	
6				5	

Puzzle #15

6x6 Sudoku

			1	2	
1	2				
3	5	4	6		2
6		2		3	5
	4	6		5	1
5		1		6	

Puzzle #16

6x6 Sudoku

2	5	6	1	4	
4		1			
3		2			5
					2
1	6	3	5		
5	2	4		6	1

Puzzle #17

6x6 Sudoku

	2			4	
	4		6		3
					6
	6	3		5	2
		5			4
	3	4	2	1	

Puzzle #18

6x6 Sudoku

2	6	3		1	4
	4			2	
	2	1		4	
4	5	6	1		
6	3	4	2	5	
				6	3

Puzzle #19

6x6 Sudoku

	3			2	1
1				5	6
	5			1	4
			5	3	
5	4	1		6	
3					

Puzzle #20

6x6 Sudoku

	5	4	6		
	3	6	4	5	
		5		4	
		2	5		
	2				4
4		3			5

Puzzle #21

6x6 Sudoku

		1		4	6
	5				2
	1		2	5	
3	2				1
		2		3	4
1			6		

Puzzle #22

6x6 Sudoku

5	2	3	4		6
		1	3	2	
2	3		6		
		5			4
	5		1	6	3
3	1			4	2

Puzzle #23

6x6 Sudoku

4	1		5	2	
5	6	2	1		
	5				2
	2		3		5
		5		6	
1	4			5	3

Puzzle #24

6x6 Sudoku

			1	5	4
				6	
2	3			4	
	4		3	1	
1		3	4	2	5
4	5				

Puzzle #25

6x6 Sudoku

5			4		2
2	1	4			6
		6		2	4
3			6	5	1
	2	5	1		3
	3		2		

Puzzle #26

6x6 Sudoku

	4			2	3
		3			5
3				5	
	5	2	4	3	
2	6	5			
	3			6	

Puzzle #27

6x6 Sudoku

			1		
		6	3		
		2		3	1
4	3			2	5
1		3		4	
6	2	4		1	3

Puzzle #28

6x6 Sudoku

4	5		2		3
		6	1	4	
1	6			3	
	4		6	5	1
6					4
5		4	3		6

Puzzle #29

6x6 Sudoku

3	1	5	2		
	4	2	3	1	5
	2			3	
1	6				
4	5	1		2	
2	3	6	4	5	

Puzzle #30

6x6 Sudoku

5	3		1	6	
	1	6			
1	6	5		3	4
4		3	5	1	6
6	5			4	
	4				

Puzzle #31

6x6 Sudoku

1	5	4			
6	3	2	5		
2		3		6	
5	6	1		4	2
3		6			
4			6	2	3

Puzzle #32

6x6 Sudoku

	5	6	1	4	
4	2	1			6
	3	5			4
					5
5		2			3
6	4	3	5	2	1

Puzzle #33

6x6 Sudoku

	3				4
	2				3
6	1	2			
3		5	6	2	
2				3	
1			4		2

Puzzle #34

6x6 Sudoku

				4	
	6	4		2	
	5	6			2
		2	6	5	4
	2		4		
		1	2		5

Puzzle #35

6x6 Sudoku

5		4	2	3	6
		3	1		
	5		3	6	
	3		5	2	
		5			
1		6		5	3

Puzzle #36

6x6 Sudoku

1	6			2	
5	2			6	
				4	
6			3	1	
4		1		3	2
2		6	4	5	

Puzzle #37

6x6 Sudoku

	1	3	5		6
		5		1	
3		1			5
5		6	1	3	4
		4			2
	5	2		4	1

Puzzle #38

6x6 Sudoku

		2	1	4	
4	1				
5					
6	3	4	2	5	
1			4	6	
	4	6		1	

Puzzle #39

6x6 Sudoku

		5		4	2
6		4			
1					5
		2	4	1	6
2				6	
	6			2	1

Puzzle #40

6x6 Sudoku

2			4		
	1	4	2	3	5
3	2	6		5	4
	4		6	2	
5	6			4	
4	3			6	2

Puzzle #41

6x6 Sudoku

	2		3	5	
		5		2	1
	5	2		3	4
			5		2
	4		2	1	
		3	6		

Puzzle #42

6x6 Sudoku

		5			1
		1	3		
4	1	2			5
5			4	1	
	2	3	5		
	5	4		2	

Puzzle #43

6x6 Sudoku

				2	5
5			4	1	6
2	1			3	
3	4		1		
	5	1	2		3
	3				

Puzzle #44

6x6 Sudoku

1	3			4	6
2	6	4	3	5	
	4	1		6	
5	2				4
6			4		
4			6		5

Puzzle #45

6x6 Sudoku

3	6		4	5	1
			2	6	3
		6	5		
5					
6		1	3		5
		5	6		

Puzzle #46

6x6 Sudoku

2		4	5		
5					2
4		5		2	1
6	2	1	4		5
			2		4
			3		6

Puzzle #47

6x6 Sudoku

3	5	6		2	1
		4			6
5				6	2
	6	1	3		4
6		5	2		
4			6	1	5

Puzzle #48

6x6 Sudoku

		4		5	2
	5			4	6
1		3		6	
		6	4	1	3
				2	1
	6				

Puzzle #49

6x6 Sudoku

3		5	6	1	
6	4			2	
	6		4		
4					1
		4		5	6
		6	1	4	

Puzzle #50

6x6 Sudoku

2			4	1	6
6		1			2
5	1				3
3		6		4	
	6				
1	3		2		

Puzzle #51

6x6 Sudoku

	5				
		6	3	1	
2	3	4		5	1
6				3	2
3	4	1	5		6
5		2	1		

Puzzle #52

6x6 Sudoku

6				3	1
5	3				2
4				1	3
			4		6
1			3		4
3					5

Puzzle #53

6x6 Sudoku

	4	1		2	5
	5		4		
2		5	1		4
	6		2		3
	1		5		
5		3			

Puzzle #54

6x6 Sudoku

1		2		6	
			1		3
	1			3	4
3		4			6
2		3	6		1
	4			5	

Puzzle #55

6x6 Sudoku

6	4	2	1		3
	5	1			4
2			4		
1	3	4		2	5
4	2				6
5	1		3	4	

Puzzle #56

6x6 Sudoku

6					1
	5			3	
5			3	1	6
3		6			
	6			5	
1	2			6	3

Puzzle #57

6x6 Sudoku

		1	6		4
	4				1
6	3			2	5
5			3	4	6
		3	5		2
		5			

Puzzle #58

6x6 Sudoku

2	4				
	6	3		2	1
	2	4		5	
			2	6	
				4	
	3		6	1	5

Puzzle #59

6x6 Sudoku

		5		3	
	3	6			2
	5		3	4	
	6		5	2	1
			4	6	3
	4	3		1	5

Puzzle #60

6x6 Sudoku

1			5		
5		3	2	1	4
6		1	4		
2		4			
4				2	5
	2	5		4	

Puzzle #61

6x6 Sudoku

		4	5		
6	5			3	2
5	3		6	4	1
4	1	6	3		5
			2		
2	6		1		4

Puzzle #62

6x6 Sudoku

		1			2
		2	6		1
4	6	5	2	1	3
			4	6	5
5	2				
	3	4	5		6

Puzzle #63

6x6 Sudoku

3					
		6			
6	3	1			5
5	4	2	3	6	
4	2		1	3	
	6	3		5	4

Puzzle #64

6x6 Sudoku

4	3		2	6	
			5	3	4
	6	4		2	
2	5		4	1	
3		6		5	
5	2			4	3

Puzzle #65

6x6 Sudoku

4		2	6		
5		6	2	3	4
3	6			2	1
2	4				6
1	2		5	6	
		3			2

Puzzle #66

6x6 Sudoku

	6	2	4		1
			3		
2	5	3	1		6
4	1			2	3
6		4			
5		1	6	3	4

Puzzle #67

6x6 Sudoku

2	6		5	3	
	4	5			
	2	4		5	
		3			6
1		6		2	
4	3	2	1	6	

Puzzle #68

6x6 Sudoku

6	1	2			
	5		2		6
	3	6			
	4		6		2
4	2		1	6	
	6		5	2	4

Puzzle #69

6x6 Sudoku

	4				
	6	2	4		3
2	3		1		5
	1	5		2	
		1	5		6
	5			4	1

Puzzle #70

6x6 Sudoku

		5			6
	2	6		5	4
	6	4	5	3	
				6	
6					5
5		2	6		

Puzzle #71

6x6 Sudoku

			1	3	
	2		5		6
		4	2		1
1	6	2	4	5	
4		3	6	2	5
		6		1	

Puzzle #72

6x6 Sudoku

	2		3		1
	6	1			
	5	2	1		
	4	3			
	1		6		
5		6		1	4

Puzzle #73

6x6 Sudoku

3			6		1
	4		3	5	
6				3	
4	5	3			
5		4	1	2	3
2	3		5	6	

Puzzle #74

6x6 Sudoku

					5
	5	1	2	3	
			4	2	
	4	6		1	3
		5		4	
		2	3		1

Puzzle #75

6x6 Sudoku

4		6	1		3
2	1	3	6		
6	2	5		3	1
		1	5		
1			2		
	6		3	1	

Puzzle #76

6x6 Sudoku

1		4		5	6
5		6		1	2
3	6		5		4
4		2	1		3
		3	2		
2	4			3	1

Puzzle #77

6x6 Sudoku

	2			4	
		5		6	
5		1	4		6
	6		5		
3		6		5	
		2	6	3	1

Puzzle #78

6x6 Sudoku

2	3	4	1		
1		6			3
	2	3	5	1	4
		5		6	
5				3	1
3			2	4	5

Puzzle #79

6x6 Sudoku

		6	2	3	4
				6	1
5				4	
6				5	
	3	1		2	5
	6	5			

Puzzle #80

6x6 Sudoku

		6	3		
2	1	4	6	5	3
5	6				
	4	2		3	6
		5	1	4	

Puzzle #81

6x6 Sudoku

	6	5	3	1	4
				5	
4	3		5		
6				4	3
	2	6	4	3	

Puzzle #82

6x6 Sudoku

	6	2	3	5	1
5	1		4		
3					6
6	2	1			3
2			1		5
1	3			2	

Puzzle #83

6x6 Sudoku

2	1	5		6	
		3	2	5	
1	2		5		
	5	6		4	
5	6	1	3	2	
	3	2		1	5

Puzzle #84

6x6 Sudoku

5	1				6
	4	6		3	
				6	1
				2	
	5	4	6	1	
	2	1		5	4

Puzzle #85

6x6 Sudoku

	1	6	4	2	5
2					3
	3	2		6	
6		4	2	3	
		1		4	
4		3	1		

Puzzle #86

6x6 Sudoku

		4			2
	1		5		3
	6	2		3	5
	4			2	1
	2	5		1	4
		1	2	5	6

Puzzle #87

6x6 Sudoku

		4	2	6	
6	1	2	5	3	
1			4	5	3
	4	5	6		
4		3			6
2		1		4	5

Puzzle #88

6x6 Sudoku

3	2	6		1	
	4	1	6	2	3
	6	4		5	
		5			2
4		2	1	3	6
6	1	3			

Puzzle #89

6x6 Sudoku

			5		4
1					3
6	5		1	3	2
2					6
5		6	3	4	
	3				5

Puzzle #90

6x6 Sudoku

4	3	5	6	2	
			4	3	
3				5	4
		1	2		
				1	2
	1	3		4	6

Puzzle #91

6x6 Sudoku

3		2			4
		5	2	1	
5		3		2	6
		6			
2	3		5		
		1	3	4	

Puzzle #92

6x6 Sudoku

3		2	4	6	5
		6		2	1
6		1		4	
4		5		1	3
2	6			5	
	5				

Puzzle #93

6x6 Sudoku

6		5			
		1	4	5	
5	6	4		1	3
2	1			4	5
4			5	6	1
1				2	

Puzzle #94

6x6 Sudoku

	2				
3	1				2
		2	5		3
1	5	3			
6	3	5	2	4	1
2	4	1		6	5

Puzzle #95

6x6 Sudoku

2	1	3		4	
	5			1	
6	4			3	
5		1			
	6	4			
1	2		3	6	

Puzzle #96

6x6 Sudoku

3	1		2		6
4					5
			5	6	3
		3			1
2	3			5	4
			3	1	

Puzzle #97

6x6 Sudoku

		6		4	5
	3	5	1	6	
					6
6				1	3
			6		4
2	6			3	

Puzzle #98

6x6 Sudoku

1				6	4
		6		1	
6	5	4	1		2
	2	1	6		
4	6		3	5	
		3		2	

Puzzle #99

6x6 Sudoku

3	2		1	6	4
	4	6		2	
5	1			3	6
4	6				
		1	5		2
	5	4		1	3

Puzzle #100

6x6 Sudoku

6	1		2		
	3		4	1	6
	5		6		
4			1		
3	4		5	6	
5	6			4	

Puzzle #101

6x6 Sudoku

1	4		6	2	
				1	4
6				5	
5		3	2		
			4	6	5
4	5		1	3	2

Puzzle #102

6x6 Sudoku

		3	4		5
	2	5			3
			6	4	2
2			3	5	1
5	1		2	3	
6	3		5	1	4

Puzzle #103

6x6 Sudoku

3			5	6	4
6		4			3
		1	4		
4		3	6	5	1
2			1	4	6

Puzzle #104

6x6 Sudoku

6	2			3	
4			6		
3	4		1		
	1	6		4	5
	3	4		5	6
			4		3

Puzzle #105

6x6 Sudoku

6		5			1
	3		5	2	6
	1	6	2	5	
		4		6	
		2	6		5
5	6	3		1	

Puzzle #106

6x6 Sudoku

		1			
3			2	1	
5	1	4	6	2	3
2		3		4	1
	4	2	1	3	5
1	3				2

Puzzle #107

6x6 Sudoku

				5	
		4	1	2	3
		1	5	4	2
	2	5	3	1	6
2	5	3			
1				3	5

Puzzle #108

6x6 Sudoku

	5	2	1		6
		3		5	4
5			6	1	3
3		1			5
	3	6		4	
			3		

Puzzle #109

6x6 Sudoku

3		2	5	1	
1	5	6	3		4
	3	1		6	5
	6	5		3	1
	1	3	6		
			1		3

Puzzle #110

6x6 Sudoku

3		6	1	2	
	1				
5	3				
			5	3	2
		3	2	4	1
	2	4	3		

Puzzle #111

6x6 Sudoku

3					6
4	5	6	3		
		4	2		5
		5	1		
6	1		5	2	
	4	2	6	3	

Puzzle #112

6x6 Sudoku

	3		4		
		5	2	3	6
5	4	1		2	
		3	1		
1			3		
	6		5		

Puzzle #113

6x6 Sudoku

1	6	3	2		
		2	1		
			5		3
5	3		6		2
	2	1			5
		5			

Puzzle #114

6x6 Sudoku

5	2			1	
3	1			4	5
3	1			4	5
6	5			2	
		5			1
4	3	1	2	5	

Puzzle #115

6x6 Sudoku

	2	1	5	3	4
	4	3			
1	3			4	6
4					1
	1	4	6		
					3

Puzzle #116

6x6 Sudoku

		2			5
1	6	5	3	2	4
	5	4	2		1
		1			6
	4		5		
5	1			4	

Puzzle #117

6x6 Sudoku

4	3	1	5		2
				4	1
2	1	4	6		
	5		2	1	4
		5	4		
3	4		1		5

Puzzle #118

6x6 Sudoku

3				4	
5			6	3	1
1	3	6	4		5
	4	5			3
	1		3	5	6
			2	1	

Puzzle #119

6x6 Sudoku

2	1		3	4	6
6			5		
4	6		1	3	
		3			4
		6	4	5	1
	4	1			3

Puzzle #120

6x6 Sudoku

3		2			
6		4	3		
4	3	5	1	2	
2	6	1			3
		6	2	3	1

Puzzle #121

6x6 Sudoku

6	1				
		3		6	
		1	6	4	
4	5	6	3		
3			1	5	6
1	6				

Puzzle #122

6x6 Sudoku

5					2
1	2	4	3	5	6
					4
2	4			3	1
4		2		1	5
6	5		4		

Puzzle #123

6x6 Sudoku

	1	5			6
		6			5
				2	3
2	6	3	1		
6	4		5	3	1
5	3	1			

Puzzle #124

6x6 Sudoku

4	6		2	5	3
5	3		1	6	4
1			3	2	5
6	1				
2	5	3	4		6

Puzzle #125

6x6 Sudoku

5	1		6	3	4
	6	4		1	
	4	5	1		
1			5		2
		3		5	
4			3		

Puzzle #126

6x6 Sudoku

				2	5
2		1	4	3	
				4	3
5	4	3	6	1	2
	2				1
	1			6	4

Puzzle #127

6x6 Sudoku

	2			5	1
4		1		3	
					5
			2		
	1	3	5	6	4
	4			2	3

Puzzle #128

6x6 Sudoku

4				6	5
2		5			
1	3		5	4	
6	5		3		2
5		1	6	2	
3	2		4		1

Puzzle #129

6x6 Sudoku

6	1		3	2	4
	4				1
1					3
3		2	1	4	
4	3				
5	2	1	4		6

Puzzle #130

6x6 Sudoku

5	6	1		4	3
4					5
	4		3		2
3				5	1
		4	5	3	
			1		

Puzzle #131

6x6 Sudoku

	6			2	5
5					4
2	4				6
3				5	2
	5		2		
	3		5		1

Puzzle #132

6x6 Sudoku

5	4	6		2	
	2				
4	3		6	1	
6	1	5	3		2
	5		2	3	
2	6	3			

Puzzle #133

6x6 Sudoku

4	3	6			
		2	3	4	6
	4	3		1	
	2	5		3	
	6				
	5	1		6	2

Puzzle #134

6x6 Sudoku

3	2			5	1
					3
6		1			
	3	5	1		
	1	2	3		
	6		2	1	

Puzzle #135

6x6 Sudoku

		5	3	1	
	1	4	3		6	
		1	4		
3		4			
5	1		6	4	
			5		

Puzzle #136

6x6 Sudoku

5	2	1		3	
6	4		2	1	5
1	3	4	5	6	2
	5	6	1		3
3		2			

Puzzle #137

6x6 Sudoku

5			4	2	
4		1	3		
			2	4	5
	4				
6	1	2			4
3	5			6	2

Puzzle #138

6x6 Sudoku

5	3		1		
4				5	
2	5	1	3	4	6
3		4	5		
	2			1	
1	4		6		

Puzzle #139

6x6 Sudoku

6	4	1	2	3	
3			6	4	1
		6	4	5	
5	3		1	6	
	6	5		2	
4	2		5		

Puzzle #140

6x6 Sudoku

	4	6		5	3
5			1		
		1	4		5
		4		2	1
			5	1	
				6	2

Puzzle #141

6x6 Sudoku

	1	5	6	4	3
4					1
5	4		3		
	3			6	5
3	5		1		
6			5		4

Puzzle #142

6x6 Sudoku

2	3		4		6
4				1	2
3	1	4			
		5		3	
5	4	3	6		
	6	2	5	4	3

Puzzle #143

6x6 Sudoku

	1	4			
6	2	3	4		1
4	3				
	6	5	2	3	4
	5		3	4	6
			5		

Puzzle #144

6x6 Sudoku

		1	4		
4					1
5			2	1	6
		6	3		5
1		4		2	3
	5		1		4

Puzzle #145

6x6 Sudoku

1	5	3		2	4
4					
6	4	1			
5		2	4	1	6
		5	3	4	1
	1	4	5		2

Puzzle #146

6x6 Sudoku

	5			2	
				4	5
2	4	6	5	3	
	1		2	6	
	6	4	3		2
		3		1	6

Puzzle #147

6x6 Sudoku

4	3				
			4		
3		5	1	6	4
6	4				3
2	6		3		
5			2	4	6

Puzzle #148

6x6 Sudoku

5	4			1	3
6	1		4		5
		1	5		
4	5	6		3	
2		4			
				4	2

Puzzle #149

6x6 Sudoku

			4	3	
3		4			
	4				3
6	1	3		2	4
		1	2		
		2		4	1

Puzzle #150

6x6 Sudoku

	5				6
	6		5	1	3
	1		3	4	
2	3	4			5
3					
6		5	2	3	

Puzzle #151

6x6 Sudoku

6		3			
4	1	5		6	
	5	1	4		
	6		2	5	1
		6			
5	4		6		3

Puzzle #152

6x6 Sudoku

			1	5	3
1	3	5			
				3	6
		3			
	5	6	3		1
	2		5	6	4

Puzzle #153

6x6 Sudoku

6	5	1		3	
3	2		1	6	
5	6			1	
		3			
1			2	5	
2	3	5		4	

Puzzle #154

6x6 Sudoku

	3	2	5		
	5			1	3
		1		3	
5		3	4	2	
3		5	1	4	6
4	1	6	3		2

Puzzle #155

6x6 Sudoku

6	4			5	
3			1	6	
			6		5
1	5		3		
	6			3	
4	1		5		

Puzzle #156

6x6 Sudoku

	4	1			2
2	6			4	
4		6	1	5	3
	1		4	2	
	5	2	3		4
6	3			1	5

Puzzle #157

6x6 Sudoku

2			1	3	4
1			2	6	5
4	6	3			1
5		1	3	4	
3					2

Puzzle #158

6x6 Sudoku

4	1			2	5
	5	2			
2			1		4
			5		2
6	4	1		5	3
5	2	3		1	

Puzzle #159

6x6 Sudoku

	1	2		5	4
		6		2	1
		1	4		6
	3				2
1	6				5
		5			

Puzzle #160

6x6 Sudoku

5		4		2	1
2		1	6	4	5
	2				4
3					
6				5	2
4		2		6	

Puzzle #161

6x6 Sudoku

	6	1	3	5	
3				2	
		5	6		
6		2		1	5
	1		2	4	
	2	3	5		

Puzzle #162

6x6 Sudoku

	1		5	6	3
3	5				1
	2		3		6
	3			2	
					5
5	4		6	1	2

Puzzle #163

6x6 Sudoku

	3	5			2
	2	6	5	4	
		3		6	5
	5				4
	1		4		6
	6	4			

Puzzle #164

6x6 Sudoku

				3	2
3		4	1	6	
4			6	2	
6		2		4	1
1		3			6
		5			4

Puzzle #165

6x6 Sudoku

1	6	2	4	5	3
			1	6	
5		6	3		
			5	2	
6		1			
2	3		6	1	

Puzzle #166

6x6 Sudoku

1			6		4
4	6	3	5		1
5		6	1	4	2
2			3	5	
3		1		6	
			2	1	3

Puzzle #167

6x6 Sudoku

2	6		1		
	1				6
	5	6			4
	3				
6	2	5	4		3
	4	1	5	6	

Puzzle #168

6x6 Sudoku

				4	2
5	1		2	3	
	3	6	4	5	1
6	2	5	3	1	4
		3		2	

Puzzle #169

6x6 Sudoku

5	3	6		4	
	1		3		
4	5	2			3
		1	5	2	4
6					
1		5	6		

Puzzle #170

6x6 Sudoku

				5	2
3	5		6		4
	2			4	6
		4	2	3	
			5	2	3
2		5			1

Puzzle #171

6x6 Sudoku

	4	2			
5	3		2	6	
2		3	6	4	
1		4	3	5	
	1		4		
4	2	6	5	1	

Puzzle #172

6x6 Sudoku

	3		1	6	
	4		3	5	2
3	2		4		5
4			6	2	
	5		2	4	6
2			5		1

Puzzle #173

6x6 Sudoku

	2	3	1	4	5
1	5		3	6	
5		6	2	1	4
2		1			
3	6		4		
4			5		6

Puzzle #174

6x6 Sudoku

		4		3	2
5		2	1		6
	5	6	3	1	4
3	4	1			
			4		1
				6	3

Puzzle #175

6x6 Sudoku

5		4	1		
	1	3			
				6	
2		5	3	4	1
3			2	1	4
	4	2			3

Puzzle #176

6x6 Sudoku

			4	3	1
4	1		2		5
1	3			5	
2					
	2		5	4	
6					3

Puzzle #177

6x6 Sudoku

		2	3		
4	6			1	2
3	4				
6			1		
2	3		4		
1		4	6		3

Puzzle #178

6x6 Sudoku

	4		2	5	
2					3
		4		2	1
1		5			4
	1	3		4	2
4	6	2	1		5

Puzzle #179

6x6 Sudoku

	4	5		6	1
		3			5
		2	4		6
4		6			
					4
3	6	4		1	

Puzzle #180

6x6 Sudoku

3		1	6	5	4
4		5			
				6	5
6	5		3		
5			2	4	
					3

Puzzle #181

6x6 Sudoku

		3	4	5	
				1	
2		5	1		4
1	4		3	2	
	2			4	
5		4	2		

Puzzle #182

6x6 Sudoku

3	2				5
	4			3	2
	6			5	1
	1	3	2	4	6
2	5	4	1		3
			5	2	

Puzzle #183

6x6 Sudoku

5	6			1	3
2	1			5	
4	5	1			
					5
	4	5		2	
			5	6	4

Puzzle #184

6x6 Sudoku

	6		3		1
		3		6	
			4	5	3
4				2	
6	2	1	5		
	5		6	1	

Puzzle #185

6x6 Sudoku

	5				
1				3	5
4		6		2	3
3	2				
6		1	4	5	2
5	4				1

Puzzle #186

6x6 Sudoku

4		3	6	2	1
1	6	2	3	4	5
	1	4			
		5	1		4
5			4	6	
	4			1	3

Puzzle #187

6x6 Sudoku

	4	1			5
2			4	1	
4		3	1	5	6
		4			1
6			5		4

Puzzle #188

6x6 Sudoku

		1			6
6		3	4		1
	3			1	
	5			6	3
3	6	2		4	5
4	1	5			2

Puzzle #189

6x6 Sudoku

5	6		2	3	1
1					
			3	5	
				6	
		1		2	5
2	5		4	1	

Puzzle #190

6x6 Sudoku

1	4	2			
6			4		
3		5	1		4
		1	5		6
2	3	4	6	5	
				4	

Puzzle #191

6x6 Sudoku

	1		3	6	
3	6	4			
1				2	3
6	2	3		4	
2	5		4	3	
4			2	1	

Puzzle #192

6x6 Sudoku

	3	2	5		6
		6		3	2
	6		2		5
	5		3	6	4
		5		2	
6	2			5	1

Puzzle #193

6x6 Sudoku

3			1	6	2
	1	6	3	5	4
5	6		4		
4	3	1			5
1	5		2	4	
6	2				

Puzzle #194

6x6 Sudoku

					5
			1	2	3
1		4			6
3	5		4	1	2
		2	3	5	
		1	2		4

Puzzle #195

6x6 Sudoku

2	1	4			
5					
	3			5	
4	5		2	1	
6	4				2
	2	1	5		6

Puzzle #196

6x6 Sudoku

	3	5			
6	1		5		4
1			3		
2	5				6
3	4	6		5	2
			6		3

Puzzle #197

6x6 Sudoku

5		4	6	1	
	6		5		
		5			
6	4		3		1
1	5		4	2	6
	2				5

Puzzle #198

6x6 Sudoku

	5				6
		1		2	5
			5		1
1	4	5	6		
		4	1	5	3
5			2		4

Puzzle #199

6x6 Sudoku

2	1				
6		3	2		
3	5			4	6
			5		
			6	2	4
	2	6	3	5	

Puzzle #200

6x6 Sudoku

	1	4		6	
3	6		4		1
	4	3	1		2
	2	1	3		
1	5		2		4
	3	2	6	1	

Puzzle #201

6x6 Sudoku

		4			1
1	5	6		2	
		5	1		3
	1		2		6
			4	1	
5		1			2

Puzzle #202

6x6 Sudoku

6		5	3	1	
	1	4			2	
3	1	4			
2	5	6	4	3	
4	3		6	5	2
			1	4	

Puzzle #203

6x6 Sudoku

				3	5
2			4		
5		4	1		2
1			3	2	4
4			5	1	6

Puzzle #204

6x6 Sudoku

	6		3		
5		2	1		
2		4			
	5		4		2
	2		6	3	4
6	4	3			

Puzzle #205

6x6 Sudoku

	6		5		
5	3			4	
3					
4	1	6	2	3	5
2	5		4		6
6	4			5	2

Puzzle #206

6x6 Sudoku

	6				1
	4		3	5	
5				6	4
6			5		2
2		1			5
	5		2	1	3

Puzzle #207

6x6 Sudoku

1		2	6		
		5		2	4
4	6	1	2		3
5		3			
		4		6	
3	1	6	5		

Puzzle #208

6x6 Sudoku

2	3		6	5	
5				2	3
4	2		1	6	
		6		4	2
6	1		2		4
	4	2			

Puzzle #209

6x6 Sudoku

4		1	6	5	2
5	2	6	3		4
6			2		
		3			6
		2		6	
	6	4	1	2	5

Puzzle #210

6x6 Sudoku

		2	4		
4		6	2	5	
6	4	5	1		
1		3			5
2	3			1	

Puzzle #211

6x6 Sudoku

	6	4	3		1
1		5	2		4
				4	
6				1	2
			1	3	6
3	1		4	2	5

Puzzle #212

6x6 Sudoku

3		1		2	4
2	4	5	6		1
	3		1	5	
	1	6		4	
1	2	4			
	5		4	1	2

Puzzle #213

6x6 Sudoku

3	6				
1	5		2		3
2	4		3		
6	1	3	4	2	5
				3	4
4		6		5	

Puzzle #214

6x6 Sudoku

				2	1
	3	2	4		6
	6	4	1	3	5
	1				4
			6	4	
		3		1	2

Puzzle #215

6x6 Sudoku

1	4	3			
6	2	5	1		4
4	1	2	3		6
	5	6	4	2	1
5					2
			5		

Puzzle #216

6x6 Sudoku

6	4	5		3	
		3		6	
2		6	4	5	
					6
	6		3	4	2
		2	6		

Puzzle #217

6x6 Sudoku

4	5	2		3	6
	1		4		2
5	3		2		
2	6		3		
			5		1
1	4		6	2	

Puzzle #218

6x6 Sudoku

		4	1		
5					
3	5	2			
	1	6	3	5	
		3	5		4
2			6		3

Puzzle #219

6x6 Sudoku

4				1	3
6	3			2	5
	6	4	3	5	
			2		6
	1				
5	4	6		3	

Puzzle #220

6x6 Sudoku

	4	3	1	6	5
		6		2	
			6		
6			2		4
5	1		3		
3	6		5	1	2

Puzzle #221

6x6 Sudoku

	3		4	5	
	2	5			
4		3	2		5
2	5	1		4	
3		4	5	2	

Puzzle #222

6x6 Sudoku

	4	1			
2	5	3			6
1	3	4		5	2
5	6	2	3		
4	1				
		5	4	6	1

Puzzle #223

6x6 Sudoku

		1	4		
4	3	5		2	1
				6	3
6	1	3	2		
1				4	6
3	4	6			

Puzzle #224

6x6 Sudoku

4	2		6		
5	6		2		
	1		3	5	
	4	5		2	
6	3	4	5	1	2
1	5		4		3

Puzzle #225

6x6 Sudoku

2		4	1		5
	3	1	2		
			4	2	
4	1		6	5	
1	4	5	3		
3	2	6			4

Puzzle #226

6x6 Sudoku

4		3		1	
5	1	2	3		4
3	5	4	6		
6			4		
	3			4	5
2		5			

Puzzle #227

6x6 Sudoku

2	6	1	3	4	5
4	3	5			
3	4		2	5	
	1		5	2	4
5	2		6		

Puzzle #228

6x6 Sudoku

2				6	4
3	6		5		1
5			1	3	2
1				4	
		3		5	
				1	3

Puzzle #229

6x6 Sudoku

2			4		5
		4	2		1
					6
6	4			1	2
				2	4
4	1				3

Puzzle #230

6x6 Sudoku

1		6	2	5	4
5	4	2		6	
2	1	5			
4			5	2	
				4	
3			6		2

Puzzle #231

6x6 Sudoku

6	3	1	4		2
	4			1	
		3	2	4	5
4				6	
3		6		2	
2	5	4			

Puzzle #232

6x6 Sudoku

	3	2			
6	5		2	4	
	4	6		5	2
5		3	1	6	4
3	6	5			
	1	4	6		5

Puzzle #233

6x6 Sudoku

			3	5	
6	3	5		4	2
5		3	6	1	
4			2		
		6			
3	5	2			

Puzzle #234

6x6 Sudoku

5	2	4	1	3	
			4		
	5			1	4
4			2	5	
2	4			6	1
6	1	5	3	4	

Puzzle #235

6x6 Sudoku

	4		1	6	5
					3
	5	4		3	1
		2		4	
5	2			1	4
	3	1			

Puzzle #236

6x6 Sudoku

			2		6
3	2	6	5	4	
	5	3			2
	4			1	5
	3	1	6		4
2	6				

Puzzle #237

6x6 Sudoku

	2		3	4	1
	4	3	2	6	
2	5		4	1	
4	3	1	5		6
	1		6		
	6	4			2

Puzzle #238

6x6 Sudoku

5			4	1	6
4		6	3		5
3	6		1		
	2	4			3
2		3	6	5	
	5	1			4

Puzzle #239

6x6 Sudoku

5	2			1	3
		4	2	5	6
6				3	
3		2			
			6	2	
2	6				1

Puzzle #240

6x6 Sudoku

3		1			
6					4
2		5	3		
4	3	6	5		1
1	2	3	4	6	5
		4	2		

Puzzle #241

6x6 Sudoku

			2	5	
6				4	
	1	4		2	5
2			4	1	3
			5		
	4	3	1	6	2

Puzzle #242

6x6 Sudoku

6	2	3	1	4	5
		5		6	3
3			6	5	
5		2	4		
				1	4
1		4			

Puzzle #243

6x6 Sudoku

				6	2
1	6		4	3	5
	5	3	6		1
6	4		2	5	
3	2		5	1	
5					

Puzzle #244

6x6 Sudoku

5	4		2	3	
3			4		1
				4	
4	2	6		1	3
2	1		3		5
6		3		2	

Puzzle #245

6x6 Sudoku

2	4	3		5	6
	5			2	3
		4		1	
	1		2		4
5		2	6	4	1
4			5	3	2

Puzzle #246

6x6 Sudoku

		3	6		5
4				3	
6	4		5	1	
		1		6	2
5		6	1		
		4			6

Puzzle #247

6x6 Sudoku

4				6	3
		6	2	1	
	6	5		3	1
	2				6
6	5	1	3	4	2

Puzzle #248

6x6 Sudoku

		6		5	1
	1	5		4	6
1		2		3	
	6	3	5		
6				2	5
		1	4	6	

Puzzle #249

6x6 Sudoku

		2		4	6
		6		1	
4	5	1	6	3	2
		3	1		4
1			3	2	5
		5	4	6	1

Puzzle #250

6x6 Sudoku

3		5	4	1	6
		1			
1			2		5
2		4	6	3	1
5		3	1	6	
6			3	5	4

Puzzle #251

6x6 Sudoku

	5	4		1	2
3			4		6
1	3			4	
		5		3	1
2		3		6	4
5			1		3

Puzzle #252

6x6 Sudoku

3	4	2	6		5
5			4	3	2
6	5	1	3	2	
			5		1
			2	4	3
	3		1	5	

Puzzle #253

6x6 Sudoku

	5	3	2	4	
4	2	1			
3	4			1	2
			5	3	
	6	4			
1		2	4		5

Puzzle #254

6x6 Sudoku

2			4	1	
4	1		2	3	6
5	2	1	6		
		3	5		
1	6	4		5	
	5	2		6	4

Puzzle #255

6x6 Sudoku

3				5	2
	4		3		1
	2	4			5
6	5	3	2		4
	1	6			
2	3				

Puzzle #256

6x6 Sudoku

		1		4	5
4		6	2		3
2		5	3		4
6				5	2
	4	2	5		
		3	4	2	

Puzzle #257

6x6 Sudoku

		3			4
4	1	2		6	3
	5	4	6		2
	3		1	4	
3	2				6
6	4	5	3		1

Puzzle #258

6x6 Sudoku

		4	3	5	6
	6	5			4
5	4	2	6		1
		1	2		
1		3	4	6	2
4		6			

Puzzle #259

6x6 Sudoku

3	5	1	4		2
6	2	4			
				1	
	3		2	4	
4		2		5	3
	6			2	4

Puzzle #260

6x6 Sudoku

	3	5	6		1
6	2			5	
					3
1	5	3		6	2
3	1		2		5
	4				

Puzzle #261

6x6 Sudoku

		1	5		
	5	2		3	
3	6		1		2
2			3	5	6
	2				
1	4	3	2	6	5

Puzzle #262

6x6 Sudoku

6		3			2
5					6
			2	4	5
	5	4		6	
	6	5	3		1
3	1			5	4

Puzzle #263

6x6 Sudoku

2				6	5
	6	5	3			
	3		4		6
	6	2			
			6		
	4		1	5	2

Puzzle #264

6x6 Sudoku

4			1		
3	5		2	4	6
2		3			
6		5	3		
5	3	2		6	1
1	6			3	

Puzzle #265

6x6 Sudoku

5	2				6
	6			4	5
	4	6		3	
		3	4		
4	1	2			
6	3			2	

Puzzle #266

6x6 Sudoku

1	4			2	
		2	1	3	
3				6	2
4	2	6	3	5	1
	3		5		6
	6		2		3

Puzzle #267

6x6 Sudoku

				5	
2	5	4			
3			4	2	5
				3	1
4	3	1		6	2
6			1	4	

Puzzle #268

6x6 Sudoku

	3	1	2		4
	5	4	3	1	6
		2	5	6	
5	6	3		4	2
	1				
4		5	6	3	

Puzzle #269

6x6 Sudoku

	3		5	6	
1	5				4
6		5		4	
	2	4			
	6	1	4	3	
		3		5	6

Puzzle #270

6x6 Sudoku

2		1		4	
3	5	4	1	2	
	1		3	5	4
					1
			2	3	5

Puzzle #271

6x6 Sudoku

		2			6
				2	
		6	2	3	4
4	2	3	6	1	
5	3		4	6	
2	6	4			

Puzzle #272

6x6 Sudoku

6	2			1	3
	3			2	
2				4	
		3	2	6	5
1					
	4	2	1		

Puzzle #273

6x6 Sudoku

5				2	
6	3		1	5	4
3				4	
	6	4	5		
	2	3			
	5			3	1

Puzzle #274

6x6 Sudoku

3	2	4			
5			3		
4		3	1		2
				6	
6	4	2			
		5	2	4	6

Puzzle #275

6x6 Sudoku

				1	
1	3	2		4	
6			2	5	
5	2		1		
3	5			2	1
		1		6	

Puzzle #276

6x6 Sudoku

		3		6	2
6		2	4		3
		1		5	4
5	6				
4	2	6			
	1	5	2		6

Puzzle #277

6x6 Sudoku

	6	2		4	3
	3	1	2		6
6				1	
2	1	5			
		6			1
1			6	3	

Puzzle #278

6x6 Sudoku

	4		5		3
	5				1
5			6	1	2
6	1		3	5	
4	6	3		2	
	2	5		3	

Puzzle #279

6x6 Sudoku

5	1		4		
	4		3		5
	6	5	1		4
4	3	1	2	5	6
3		6			
1		4		2	3

Puzzle #280

6x6 Sudoku

		5		1	
			4	6	
2	3		5		1
5	1			2	
6			1	5	2
	5		6	3	4

Puzzle #281

6x6 Sudoku

5			3		1
			5	6	2
6	5		1	2	
			6		3
1	4	5	2		
		2	4		5

Puzzle #282

6x6 Sudoku

2		3	5	1	
6		1	2	3	4
		5		2	
1	2	4		5	
4		2	1		5
5	1			4	

Puzzle #283

6x6 Sudoku

	6				3
3		4	6	2	1
5		3	1		
4	1	6	5	3	
	4		3	6	
	3	5	2		

Puzzle #284

6x6 Sudoku

	2	5			
4	3	6			
5					4
2					
3	4	1			5
6	5		3	4	1

Puzzle #285

6x6 Sudoku

6			1		
	1	5			6
5					4
	3	4		5	
3			2		1
	2	1			3

Puzzle #286

6x6 Sudoku

	1	6			
4	3	2		5	
		5	1		2
		1		6	5
1	5			4	
2		4		1	3

Puzzle #287

6x6 Sudoku

		4		2	
	5		4	3	
	1		2	4	6
	2		5		3
	4	1	3	6	2
			1	5	

Puzzle #288

6x6 Sudoku

	2		3	6	
			2		
1		6		3	
		4	6	1	
	1	2		4	
3	4	5		2	

Puzzle #289

6x6 Sudoku

4	3	1	2		
	5			4	
1	4		6	5	2
5		2		3	4
			4	2	
3	2	4	5	1	

Puzzle #290

6x6 Sudoku

		4		1	5
	1		2	4	
2		1	5		4
		3		2	
			3		1
		6	4		2

Puzzle #291

6x6 Sudoku

		6		3	2
2	4	3	1	5	
					1
	6	1	3	2	5
6	2	4		1	
3		5	2	6	

Puzzle #292

6x6 Sudoku

		3		4	1
			2	6	
		6	1	2	
2					6
			6	1	
	6	2		3	

Puzzle #293

6x6 Sudoku

2	1		6	5	4
		4		2	3
		2	5	3	6
			4	1	2
	6	5			1
4	2			6	5

Puzzle #294

6x6 Sudoku

4	6	3	1	2	
	1				
	4	1		5	3
3	5	2		1	4
1	3		5	4	2
				6	

Puzzle #295

6x6 Sudoku

5		6	3	4	
			6		2
2			1		6
	6				5
3		2			
6		4	2		

Puzzle #296

6x6 Sudoku

		6		3	
4	2	3		5	6
2			6	4	5
6	4		3	1	2
3	6		5		
	5				

Puzzle #297

6x6 Sudoku

		3		6	
5		2		3	1
2	5				4
4					2
	2	5	1		3
	1	4	5		6

Puzzle #298

6x6 Sudoku

		4	1	6	
3	6	1		5	
5				4	6
4	2			3	1
	4	2			5
1	3			2	

Puzzle #299

6x6 Sudoku

5			3		6
				4	5
	2				3
6	5	3			4
4		5	6		2
2	3				1

Puzzle #300

6x6 Sudoku

	5	1		3	
6			5	1	
	1	6		2	3
			1		
			3		
3	4		2	6	1

Puzzle #1

3	6	1	5	2	4
4	2	5	1	3	6
5	4	3	2	6	1
2	1	6	4	5	3
6	5	4	3	1	2
1	3	2	6	4	5

Puzzle #2

6	4	3	1	2	5
1	5	2	3	4	6
5	2	1	4	6	3
3	6	4	2	5	1
4	3	6	5	1	2
2	1	5	6	3	4

Puzzle #3

4	5	3	1	2	6
1	6	2	5	4	3
3	1	5	2	6	4
2	4	6	3	1	5
6	3	1	4	5	2
5	2	4	6	3	1

Puzzle #4

5	4	3	2	1	6
1	2	6	3	4	5
2	3	5	4	6	1
4	6	1	5	2	3
3	1	4	6	5	2
6	5	2	1	3	4

Puzzle #5

2	4	5	1	3	6
3	1	6	2	5	4
4	5	1	3	6	2
6	2	3	5	4	1
5	6	2	4	1	3
1	3	4	6	2	5

Puzzle #6

5	2	6	4	3	1
3	1	4	2	6	5
2	6	3	5	1	4
4	5	1	3	2	6
6	4	2	1	5	3
1	3	5	6	4	2

Puzzle #7

2	5	1	6	3	4
6	4	3	1	2	5
3	6	4	2	5	1
5	1	2	4	6	3
4	2	5	3	1	6
1	3	6	5	4	2

Puzzle #8

4	5	2	6	1	3
3	6	1	5	4	2
5	4	3	2	6	1
1	2	6	3	5	4
2	1	5	4	3	6
6	3	4	1	2	5

Puzzle #9

5	1	6	2	4	3
3	4	2	1	5	6
2	5	4	6	3	1
6	3	1	5	2	4
1	2	3	4	6	5
4	6	5	3	1	2

Puzzle #10

1	4	6	5	3	2
3	2	5	1	6	4
4	1	2	6	5	3
5	6	3	2	4	1
2	5	4	3	1	6
6	3	1	4	2	5

Puzzle #11

5	3	1	6	4	2
4	6	2	1	5	3
1	2	3	4	6	5
6	4	5	2	3	1
2	5	6	3	1	4
3	1	4	5	2	6

Puzzle #12

5	1	4	2	3	6
2	6	3	4	1	5
1	5	6	3	2	4
3	4	2	5	6	1
4	3	1	6	5	2
6	2	5	1	4	3

Puzzle #13

2	3	4	1	5	6
5	6	1	3	4	2
4	1	5	6	2	3
6	2	3	4	1	5
3	4	2	5	6	1
1	5	6	2	3	4

Puzzle #14

4	2	6	5	1	3
1	3	5	4	2	6
3	5	4	1	6	2
2	6	1	3	4	5
5	1	2	6	3	4
6	4	3	2	5	1

Puzzle #15

4	6	5	1	2	3
1	2	3	5	4	6
3	5	4	6	1	2
6	1	2	4	3	5
2	4	6	3	5	1
5	3	1	2	6	4

Puzzle #16

2	5	6	1	4	3
4	3	1	2	5	6
3	4	2	6	1	5
6	1	5	4	3	2
1	6	3	5	2	4
5	2	4	3	6	1

Puzzle #17

3	2	6	5	4	1
5	4	1	6	2	3
1	5	2	4	3	6
4	6	3	1	5	2
2	1	5	3	6	4
6	3	4	2	1	5

Puzzle #18

2	6	3	5	1	4
1	4	5	3	2	6
3	2	1	6	4	5
4	5	6	1	3	2
6	3	4	2	5	1
5	1	2	4	6	3

Puzzle #19

6	3	5	4	2	1
1	2	4	3	5	6
2	5	3	6	1	4
4	1	6	5	3	2
5	4	1	2	6	3
3	6	2	1	4	5

Puzzle #20

2	5	4	6	1	3
1	3	6	4	5	2
3	1	5	2	4	6
6	4	2	5	3	1
5	2	1	3	6	4
4	6	3	1	2	5

Puzzle #21

2	3	1	5	4	6
6	5	4	3	1	2
4	1	6	2	5	3
3	2	5	4	6	1
5	6	2	1	3	4
1	4	3	6	2	5

Puzzle #22

5	2	3	4	1	6
6	4	1	3	2	5
2	3	4	6	5	1
1	6	5	2	3	4
4	5	2	1	6	3
3	1	6	5	4	2

Puzzle #23

4	1	3	5	2	6
5	6	2	1	3	4
3	5	4	6	1	2
6	2	1	3	4	5
2	3	5	4	6	1
1	4	6	2	5	3

Puzzle #24

3	2	6	1	5	4
5	1	4	2	6	3
2	3	1	5	4	6
6	4	5	3	1	2
1	6	3	4	2	5
4	5	2	6	3	1

Puzzle #25

5	6	3	4	1	2
2	1	4	5	3	6
1	5	6	3	2	4
3	4	2	6	5	1
6	2	5	1	4	3
4	3	1	2	6	5

Puzzle #26

5	4	6	1	2	3
1	2	3	6	4	5
3	1	4	2	5	6
6	5	2	4	3	1
2	6	5	3	1	4
4	3	1	5	6	2

Puzzle #27

3	4	5	1	6	2
2	1	6	3	5	4
5	6	2	4	3	1
4	3	1	6	2	5
1	5	3	2	4	6
6	2	4	5	1	3

Puzzle #28

4	5	1	2	6	3
2	3	6	1	4	5
1	6	5	4	3	2
3	4	2	6	5	1
6	1	3	5	2	4
5	2	4	3	1	6

Puzzle #29

3	1	5	2	6	4
6	4	2	3	1	5
5	2	4	1	3	6
1	6	3	5	4	2
4	5	1	6	2	3
2	3	6	4	5	1

Puzzle #30

5	3	4	1	6	2
2	1	6	4	5	3
1	6	5	2	3	4
4	2	3	5	1	6
6	5	2	3	4	1
3	4	1	6	2	5

Puzzle #31

1	5	4	2	3	6
6	3	2	5	1	4
2	4	3	1	6	5
5	6	1	3	4	2
3	2	6	4	5	1
4	1	5	6	2	3

Puzzle #32

3	5	6	1	4	2
4	2	1	3	5	6
2	3	5	6	1	4
1	6	4	2	3	5
5	1	2	4	6	3
6	4	3	5	2	1

Puzzle #33

5	3	1	2	6	4
4	2	6	5	1	3
6	1	2	3	4	5
3	4	5	6	2	1
2	5	4	1	3	6
1	6	3	4	5	2

Puzzle #34

2	1	3	5	4	6
5	6	4	1	2	3
4	5	6	3	1	2
1	3	2	6	5	4
3	2	5	4	6	1
6	4	1	2	3	5

Puzzle #35

5	1	4	2	3	6
2	6	3	1	4	5
4	5	2	3	6	1
6	3	1	5	2	4
3	4	5	6	1	2
1	2	6	4	5	3

Puzzle #36

1	6	4	5	2	3
5	2	3	1	6	4
3	1	5	2	4	6
6	4	2	3	1	5
4	5	1	6	3	2
2	3	6	4	5	1

Puzzle #37

4	1	3	5	2	6
2	6	5	4	1	3
3	4	1	2	6	5
5	2	6	1	3	4
1	3	4	6	5	2
6	5	2	3	4	1

Puzzle #38

3	6	2	1	4	5
4	1	5	3	2	6
5	2	1	6	3	4
6	3	4	2	5	1
1	5	3	4	6	2
2	4	6	5	1	3

Puzzle #39

3	1	5	6	4	2
6	2	4	1	5	3
1	4	6	2	3	5
5	3	2	4	1	6
2	5	1	3	6	4
4	6	3	5	2	1

Puzzle #40

2	5	3	4	1	6
6	1	4	2	3	5
3	2	6	1	5	4
1	4	5	6	2	3
5	6	2	3	4	1
4	3	1	5	6	2

Puzzle #41

4	2	1	3	5	6
3	6	5	4	2	1
6	5	2	1	3	4
1	3	4	5	6	2
5	4	6	2	1	3
2	1	3	6	4	5

Puzzle #42

3	6	5	2	4	1
2	4	1	3	5	6
4	1	2	6	3	5
5	3	6	4	1	2
1	2	3	5	6	4
6	5	4	1	2	3

Puzzle #43

1	6	4	3	2	5
5	2	3	4	1	6
2	1	6	5	3	4
3	4	5	1	6	2
6	5	1	2	4	3
4	3	2	6	5	1

Puzzle #44

1	3	5	2	4	6
2	6	4	3	5	1
3	4	1	5	6	2
5	2	6	1	3	4
6	5	2	4	1	3
4	1	3	6	2	5

Puzzle #45

3	6	2	4	5	1
1	5	4	2	6	3
4	1	6	5	3	2
5	2	3	1	4	6
6	4	1	3	2	5
2	3	5	6	1	4

Puzzle #46

2	1	4	5	6	3
5	6	3	1	4	2
4	3	5	6	2	1
6	2	1	4	3	5
3	5	6	2	1	4
1	4	2	3	5	6

Puzzle #47

3	5	6	4	2	1
1	2	4	5	3	6
5	4	3	1	6	2
2	6	1	3	5	4
6	1	5	2	4	3
4	3	2	6	1	5

Puzzle #48

6	1	4	3	5	2
3	5	2	1	4	6
1	4	3	2	6	5
5	2	6	4	1	3
4	3	5	6	2	1
2	6	1	5	3	4

Puzzle #49

3	2	5	6	1	4
6	4	1	5	2	3
1	6	2	4	3	5
4	5	3	2	6	1
2	1	4	3	5	6
5	3	6	1	4	2

Puzzle #50

2	5	3	4	1	6
6	4	1	3	5	2
5	1	4	6	2	3
3	2	6	1	4	5
4	6	2	5	3	1
1	3	5	2	6	4

Puzzle #51

1	5	3	2	6	4
4	2	6	3	1	5
2	3	4	6	5	1
6	1	5	4	3	2
3	4	1	5	2	6
5	6	2	1	4	3

Puzzle #52

6	2	4	5	3	1
5	3	1	6	4	2
4	5	6	2	1	3
2	1	3	4	5	6
1	6	5	3	2	4
3	4	2	1	6	5

Puzzle #53

6	4	1	3	2	5
3	5	2	4	1	6
2	3	5	1	6	4
1	6	4	2	5	3
4	1	6	5	3	2
5	2	3	6	4	1

Puzzle #54

1	3	2	4	6	5
4	6	5	1	2	3
5	1	6	2	3	4
3	2	4	5	1	6
2	5	3	6	4	1
6	4	1	3	5	2

Puzzle #55

6	4	2	1	5	3
3	5	1	2	6	4
2	6	5	4	3	1
1	3	4	6	2	5
4	2	3	5	1	6
5	1	6	3	4	2

Puzzle #56

6	3	4	5	2	1
2	5	1	6	3	4
5	4	2	3	1	6
3	1	6	2	4	5
4	6	3	1	5	2
1	2	5	4	6	3

Puzzle #57

2	5	1	6	3	4
3	4	6	2	5	1
6	3	4	1	2	5
5	1	2	3	4	6
4	6	3	5	1	2
1	2	5	4	6	3

Puzzle #58

2	4	1	5	3	6
5	6	3	4	2	1
6	2	4	1	5	3
3	1	5	2	6	4
1	5	6	3	4	2
4	3	2	6	1	5

Puzzle #59

1	2	5	6	3	4
4	3	6	1	5	2
2	5	1	3	4	6
3	6	4	5	2	1
5	1	2	4	6	3
6	4	3	2	1	5

Puzzle #60

1	4	2	5	6	3
5	6	3	2	1	4
6	3	1	4	5	2
2	5	4	6	3	1
4	1	6	3	2	5
3	2	5	1	4	6

Puzzle #61

3	2	4	5	1	6
6	5	1	4	3	2
5	3	2	6	4	1
4	1	6	3	2	5
1	4	5	2	6	3
2	6	3	1	5	4

Puzzle #62

6	4	1	3	5	2
3	5	2	6	4	1
4	6	5	2	1	3
2	1	3	4	6	5
5	2	6	1	3	4
1	3	4	5	2	6

Puzzle #63

3	5	4	6	1	2
2	1	6	5	4	3
6	3	1	4	2	5
5	4	2	3	6	1
4	2	5	1	3	6
1	6	3	2	5	4

Puzzle #64

4	3	5	2	6	1
6	1	2	5	3	4
1	6	4	3	2	5
2	5	3	4	1	6
3	4	6	1	5	2
5	2	1	6	4	3

Puzzle #65

4	3	2	6	1	5
5	1	6	2	3	4
3	6	5	4	2	1
2	4	1	3	5	6
1	2	4	5	6	3
6	5	3	1	4	2

Puzzle #66

3	6	2	4	5	1
1	4	5	3	6	2
2	5	3	1	4	6
4	1	6	5	2	3
6	3	4	2	1	5
5	2	1	6	3	4

Puzzle #67

2	6	1	5	3	4
3	4	5	6	1	2
6	2	4	3	5	1
5	1	3	2	4	6
1	5	6	4	2	3
4	3	2	1	6	5

Puzzle #68

6	1	2	3	4	5
3	5	4	2	1	6
2	3	6	4	5	1
5	4	1	6	3	2
4	2	5	1	6	3
1	6	3	5	2	4

Puzzle #69

1	4	3	6	5	2
5	6	2	4	1	3
2	3	4	1	6	5
6	1	5	3	2	4
4	2	1	5	3	6
3	5	6	2	4	1

Puzzle #70

4	3	5	1	2	6
1	2	6	3	5	4
2	6	4	5	3	1
3	5	1	4	6	2
6	4	3	2	1	5
5	1	2	6	4	3

Puzzle #71

6	4	5	1	3	2
3	2	1	5	4	6
5	3	4	2	6	1
1	6	2	4	5	3
4	1	3	6	2	5
2	5	6	3	1	4

Puzzle #72

4	2	5	3	6	1
3	6	1	4	5	2
6	5	2	1	4	3
1	4	3	5	2	6
2	1	4	6	3	5
5	3	6	2	1	4

Puzzle #73

3	2	5	6	4	1
1	4	6	3	5	2
6	1	2	4	3	5
4	5	3	2	1	6
5	6	4	1	2	3
2	3	1	5	6	4

Puzzle #74

3	2	4	1	6	5
6	5	1	2	3	4
5	1	3	4	2	6
2	4	6	5	1	3
1	3	5	6	4	2
4	6	2	3	5	1

Puzzle #75

4	5	6	1	2	3
2	1	3	6	4	5
6	2	5	4	3	1
3	4	1	5	6	2
1	3	4	2	5	6
5	6	2	3	1	4

Puzzle #76

1	2	4	3	5	6
5	3	6	4	1	2
3	6	1	5	2	4
4	5	2	1	6	3
6	1	3	2	4	5
2	4	5	6	3	1

Puzzle #77

6	2	3	1	4	5
1	4	5	3	6	2
5	3	1	4	2	6
2	6	4	5	1	3
3	1	6	2	5	4
4	5	2	6	3	1

Puzzle #78

2	3	4	1	5	6
1	5	6	4	2	3
6	2	3	5	1	4
4	1	5	3	6	2
5	4	2	6	3	1
3	6	1	2	4	5

Puzzle #79

1	5	6	2	3	4
3	4	2	5	6	1
5	2	3	1	4	6
6	1	4	3	5	2
4	3	1	6	2	5
2	6	5	4	1	3

Puzzle #80

3	5	1	2	6	4
4	2	6	3	1	5
2	1	4	6	5	3
5	6	3	4	2	1
1	4	2	5	3	6
6	3	5	1	4	2

Puzzle #81

2	6	5	3	1	4
1	4	3	6	5	2
4	3	1	5	2	6
6	5	2	1	4	3
5	2	6	4	3	1
3	1	4	2	6	5

Puzzle #82

4	6	2	3	5	1
5	1	3	4	6	2
3	5	4	2	1	6
6	2	1	5	4	3
2	4	6	1	3	5
1	3	5	6	2	4

Puzzle #83

2	1	5	4	6	3
6	4	3	2	5	1
1	2	4	5	3	6
3	5	6	1	4	2
5	6	1	3	2	4
4	3	2	6	1	5

Puzzle #84

5	1	3	2	4	6
2	4	6	1	3	5
4	3	2	5	6	1
1	6	5	4	2	3
3	5	4	6	1	2
6	2	1	3	5	4

Puzzle #85

3	1	6	4	2	5
2	4	5	6	1	3
1	3	2	5	6	4
6	5	4	2	3	1
5	6	1	3	4	2
4	2	3	1	5	6

Puzzle #86

3	5	4	1	6	2
2	1	6	5	4	3
1	6	2	4	3	5
5	4	3	6	2	1
6	2	5	3	1	4
4	3	1	2	5	6

Puzzle #87

5	3	4	2	6	1
6	1	2	5	3	4
1	2	6	4	5	3
3	4	5	6	1	2
4	5	3	1	2	6
2	6	1	3	4	5

Puzzle #88

3	2	6	5	1	4
5	4	1	6	2	3
2	6	4	3	5	1
1	3	5	4	6	2
4	5	2	1	3	6
6	1	3	2	4	5

Puzzle #89

3	6	2	5	1	4
1	4	5	6	2	3
6	5	4	1	3	2
2	1	3	4	5	6
5	2	6	3	4	1
4	3	1	2	6	5

Puzzle #90

4	3	5	6	2	1
1	6	2	4	3	5
3	2	6	1	5	4
5	4	1	2	6	3
6	5	4	3	1	2
2	1	3	5	4	6

Puzzle #91

3	1	2	6	5	4
4	6	5	2	1	3
5	4	3	1	2	6
1	2	6	4	3	5
2	3	4	5	6	1
6	5	1	3	4	2

Puzzle #92

3	1	2	4	6	5
5	4	6	3	2	1
6	3	1	5	4	2
4	2	5	6	1	3
2	6	3	1	5	4
1	5	4	2	3	6

Puzzle #93

6	4	5	1	3	2
3	2	1	4	5	6
5	6	4	2	1	3
2	1	3	6	4	5
4	3	2	5	6	1
1	5	6	3	2	4

Puzzle #94

5	2	4	1	3	6
3	1	6	4	5	2
4	6	2	5	1	3
1	5	3	6	2	4
6	3	5	2	4	1
2	4	1	3	6	5

Puzzle #95

2	1	3	6	4	5
4	5	6	2	1	3
6	4	2	5	3	1
5	3	1	4	2	6
3	6	4	1	5	2
1	2	5	3	6	4

Puzzle #96

3	1	5	2	4	6
4	2	6	1	3	5
1	4	2	5	6	3
6	5	3	4	2	1
2	3	1	6	5	4
5	6	4	3	1	2

Puzzle #97

1	2	6	3	4	5
4	3	5	1	6	2
3	4	1	2	5	6
6	5	2	4	1	3
5	1	3	6	2	4
2	6	4	5	3	1

Puzzle #98

1	3	5	2	6	4
2	4	6	5	1	3
6	5	4	1	3	2
3	2	1	6	4	5
4	6	2	3	5	1
5	1	3	4	2	6

Puzzle #99

3	2	5	1	6	4
1	4	6	3	2	5
5	1	2	4	3	6
4	6	3	2	5	1
6	3	1	5	4	2
2	5	4	6	1	3

Puzzle #100

6	1	4	2	5	3
2	3	5	4	1	6
1	5	3	6	2	4
4	2	6	1	3	5
3	4	1	5	6	2
5	6	2	3	4	1

Puzzle #101

1	4	5	6	2	3
3	6	2	5	1	4
6	2	4	3	5	1
5	1	3	2	4	6
2	3	1	4	6	5
4	5	6	1	3	2

Puzzle #102

1	6	3	4	2	5
4	2	5	1	6	3
3	5	1	6	4	2
2	4	6	3	5	1
5	1	4	2	3	6
6	3	2	5	1	4

Puzzle #103

3	1	2	5	6	4
6	5	4	2	1	3
5	6	1	4	3	2
4	2	3	6	5	1
1	4	6	3	2	5
2	3	5	1	4	6

Puzzle #104

6	2	1	5	3	4
4	5	3	6	2	1
3	4	5	1	6	2
2	1	6	3	4	5
1	3	4	2	5	6
5	6	2	4	1	3

Puzzle #105

6	2	5	3	4	1
4	3	1	5	2	6
3	1	6	2	5	4
2	5	4	1	6	3
1	4	2	6	3	5
5	6	3	4	1	2

Puzzle #106

4	2	1	3	5	6
3	5	6	2	1	4
5	1	4	6	2	3
2	6	3	5	4	1
6	4	2	1	3	5
1	3	5	4	6	2

Puzzle #107

3	1	2	6	5	4
5	6	4	1	2	3
6	3	1	5	4	2
4	2	5	3	1	6
2	5	3	4	6	1
1	4	6	2	3	5

Puzzle #108

4	5	2	1	3	6
6	1	3	2	5	4
5	2	4	6	1	3
3	6	1	4	2	5
2	3	6	5	4	1
1	4	5	3	6	2

Puzzle #109

3	4	2	5	1	6
1	5	6	3	2	4
2	3	1	4	6	5
4	6	5	2	3	1
5	1	3	6	4	2
6	2	4	1	5	3

Puzzle #110

3	4	6	1	2	5
2	1	5	4	6	3
5	3	2	6	1	4
4	6	1	5	3	2
6	5	3	2	4	1
1	2	4	3	5	6

Puzzle #111

3	2	1	4	5	6
4	5	6	3	1	2
1	3	4	2	6	5
2	6	5	1	4	3
6	1	3	5	2	4
5	4	2	6	3	1

Puzzle #112

2	3	6	4	5	1
4	1	5	2	3	6
5	4	1	6	2	3
6	2	3	1	4	5
1	5	4	3	6	2
3	6	2	5	1	4

Puzzle #113

1	6	3	2	5	4
4	5	2	1	3	6
2	1	6	5	4	3
5	3	4	6	1	2
3	2	1	4	6	5
6	4	5	3	2	1

Puzzle #114

5	2	6	3	1	4
1	4	3	5	6	2
3	1	2	6	4	5
6	5	4	1	2	3
2	6	5	4	3	1
4	3	1	2	5	6

Puzzle #115

6	2	1	5	3	4
5	4	3	1	6	2
1	3	5	2	4	6
4	6	2	3	5	1
3	1	4	6	2	5
2	5	6	4	1	3

Puzzle #116

4	3	2	1	6	5
1	6	5	3	2	4
6	5	4	2	3	1
3	2	1	4	5	6
2	4	6	5	1	3
5	1	3	6	4	2

Puzzle #117

4	3	1	5	6	2
5	6	2	3	4	1
2	1	4	6	5	3
6	5	3	2	1	4
1	2	5	4	3	6
3	4	6	1	2	5

Puzzle #118

3	6	1	5	4	2
5	2	4	6	3	1
1	3	6	4	2	5
2	4	5	1	6	3
4	1	2	3	5	6
6	5	3	2	1	4

Puzzle #119

2	1	5	3	4	6
6	3	4	5	1	2
4	6	2	1	3	5
1	5	3	2	6	4
3	2	6	4	5	1
5	4	1	6	2	3

Puzzle #120

3	1	2	4	6	5
6	5	4	3	1	2
4	3	5	1	2	6
2	6	1	5	4	3
1	2	3	6	5	4
5	4	6	2	3	1

Puzzle #121

6	1	2	5	3	4
5	4	3	2	6	1
2	3	1	6	4	5
4	5	6	3	1	2
3	2	4	1	5	6
1	6	5	4	2	3

Puzzle #122

5	6	3	1	4	2
1	2	4	3	5	6
3	1	5	2	6	4
2	4	6	5	3	1
4	3	2	6	1	5
6	5	1	4	2	3

Puzzle #123

3	1	5	2	4	6
4	2	6	3	1	5
1	5	4	6	2	3
2	6	3	1	5	4
6	4	2	5	3	1
5	3	1	4	6	2

Puzzle #124

3	2	5	6	4	1
4	6	1	2	5	3
5	3	2	1	6	4
1	4	6	3	2	5
6	1	4	5	3	2
2	5	3	4	1	6

Puzzle #125

5	1	2	6	3	4
3	6	4	2	1	5
2	4	5	1	6	3
1	3	6	5	4	2
6	2	3	4	5	1
4	5	1	3	2	6

Puzzle #126

4	3	6	1	2	5
2	5	1	4	3	6
1	6	2	5	4	3
5	4	3	6	1	2
6	2	4	3	5	1
3	1	5	2	6	4

Puzzle #127

3	2	6	4	5	1
4	5	1	6	3	2
1	6	2	3	4	5
5	3	4	2	1	6
2	1	3	5	6	4
6	4	5	1	2	3

Puzzle #128

4	1	3	2	6	5
2	6	5	1	3	4
1	3	2	5	4	6
6	5	4	3	1	2
5	4	1	6	2	3
3	2	6	4	5	1

Puzzle #129

6	1	5	3	2	4
2	4	3	6	5	1
1	5	4	2	6	3
3	6	2	1	4	5
4	3	6	5	1	2
5	2	1	4	3	6

Puzzle #130

5	6	1	2	4	3
4	3	2	6	1	5
1	4	5	3	6	2
3	2	6	4	5	1
2	1	4	5	3	6
6	5	3	1	2	4

Puzzle #131

1	6	4	3	2	5
5	2	3	6	1	4
2	4	5	1	3	6
3	1	6	4	5	2
4	5	1	2	6	3
6	3	2	5	4	1

Puzzle #132

5	4	6	1	2	3
3	2	1	5	6	4
4	3	2	6	1	5
6	1	5	3	4	2
1	5	4	2	3	6
2	6	3	4	5	1

Puzzle #133

4	3	6	5	2	1
5	1	2	3	4	6
6	4	3	2	1	5
1	2	5	6	3	4
2	6	4	1	5	3
3	5	1	4	6	2

Puzzle #134

3	2	6	4	5	1
1	5	4	6	2	3
6	4	1	5	3	2
2	3	5	1	4	6
4	1	2	3	6	5
5	6	3	2	1	4

Puzzle #135

2	6	5	3	1	4
1	4	3	2	6	5
6	5	1	4	3	2
3	2	4	1	5	6
5	1	2	6	4	3
4	3	6	5	2	1

Puzzle #136

5	2	1	6	3	4
6	4	3	2	1	5
1	3	4	5	6	2
2	6	5	3	4	1
4	5	6	1	2	3
3	1	2	4	5	6

Puzzle #137

5	6	3	4	2	1
4	2	1	3	5	6
1	3	6	2	4	5
2	4	5	6	1	3
6	1	2	5	3	4
3	5	4	1	6	2

Puzzle #138

5	3	2	1	6	4
4	1	6	2	5	3
2	5	1	3	4	6
3	6	4	5	2	1
6	2	3	4	1	5
1	4	5	6	3	2

Puzzle #139

6	4	1	2	3	5
3	5	2	6	4	1
2	1	6	4	5	3
5	3	4	1	6	2
1	6	5	3	2	4
4	2	3	5	1	6

Puzzle #140

1	4	6	2	5	3
5	3	2	1	4	6
6	2	1	4	3	5
3	5	4	6	2	1
2	6	3	5	1	4
4	1	5	3	6	2

Puzzle #141

2	1	5	6	4	3
4	6	3	2	5	1
5	4	6	3	1	2
1	3	2	4	6	5
3	5	4	1	2	6
6	2	1	5	3	4

Puzzle #142

2	3	1	4	5	6
4	5	6	3	1	2
3	1	4	2	6	5
6	2	5	1	3	4
5	4	3	6	2	1
1	6	2	5	4	3

Puzzle #143

5	1	4	6	2	3
6	2	3	4	5	1
4	3	2	1	6	5
1	6	5	2	3	4
2	5	1	3	4	6
3	4	6	5	1	2

Puzzle #144

6	3	1	4	5	2
4	2	5	6	3	1
5	4	3	2	1	6
2	1	6	3	4	5
1	6	4	5	2	3
3	5	2	1	6	4

Puzzle #145

1	5	3	6	2	4
4	2	6	1	3	5
6	4	1	2	5	3
5	3	2	4	1	6
2	6	5	3	4	1
3	1	4	5	6	2

Puzzle #146

4	5	1	6	2	3
6	3	2	1	4	5
2	4	6	5	3	1
3	1	5	2	6	4
1	6	4	3	5	2
5	2	3	4	1	6

Puzzle #147

4	3	2	6	1	5
1	5	6	4	3	2
3	2	5	1	6	4
6	4	1	5	2	3
2	6	4	3	5	1
5	1	3	2	4	6

Puzzle #148

5	4	2	6	1	3
6	1	3	4	2	5
3	2	1	5	6	4
4	5	6	2	3	1
2	3	4	1	5	6
1	6	5	3	4	2

Puzzle #149

1	5	6	4	3	2
3	2	4	1	5	6
2	4	5	6	1	3
6	1	3	5	2	4
4	3	1	2	6	5
5	6	2	3	4	1

Puzzle #150

1	5	3	4	2	6
4	6	2	5	1	3
5	1	6	3	4	2
2	3	4	1	6	5
3	2	1	6	5	4
6	4	5	2	3	1

Puzzle #151

6	2	3	1	4	5
4	1	5	3	6	2
2	5	1	4	3	6
3	6	4	2	5	1
1	3	6	5	2	4
5	4	2	6	1	3

Puzzle #152

6	4	2	1	5	3
1	3	5	6	4	2
5	1	4	2	3	6
2	6	3	4	1	5
4	5	6	3	2	1
3	2	1	5	6	4

Puzzle #153

6	5	1	4	3	2
3	2	4	1	6	5
5	6	2	3	1	4
4	1	3	5	2	6
1	4	6	2	5	3
2	3	5	6	4	1

Puzzle #154

1	3	2	5	6	4
6	5	4	2	1	3
2	4	1	6	3	5
5	6	3	4	2	1
3	2	5	1	4	6
4	1	6	3	5	2

Puzzle #155

6	4	1	2	5	3
3	2	5	1	6	4
2	3	4	6	1	5
1	5	6	3	4	2
5	6	2	4	3	1
4	1	3	5	2	6

Puzzle #156

5	4	1	6	3	2
2	6	3	5	4	1
4	2	6	1	5	3
3	1	5	4	2	6
1	5	2	3	6	4
6	3	4	2	1	5

Puzzle #157

2	5	6	1	3	4
1	3	4	2	6	5
4	6	3	5	2	1
5	2	1	3	4	6
3	4	5	6	1	2
6	1	2	4	5	3

Puzzle #158

4	1	6	3	2	5
3	5	2	6	4	1
2	3	5	1	6	4
1	6	4	5	3	2
6	4	1	2	5	3
5	2	3	4	1	6

Puzzle #159

3	1	2	6	5	4
4	5	6	3	2	1
5	2	1	4	3	6
6	3	4	5	1	2
1	6	3	2	4	5
2	4	5	1	6	3

Puzzle #160

5	6	4	3	2	1
2	3	1	6	4	5
1	2	6	5	3	4
3	4	5	2	1	6
6	1	3	4	5	2
4	5	2	1	6	3

Puzzle #161

2	6	1	3	5	4
3	5	4	1	2	6
1	4	5	6	3	2
6	3	2	4	1	5
5	1	6	2	4	3
4	2	3	5	6	1

Puzzle #162

4	1	2	5	6	3
3	5	6	2	4	1
1	2	4	3	5	6
6	3	5	1	2	4
2	6	1	4	3	5
5	4	3	6	1	2

Puzzle #163

4	3	5	6	1	2
1	2	6	5	4	3
2	4	3	1	6	5
6	5	1	2	3	4
3	1	2	4	5	6
5	6	4	3	2	1

Puzzle #164

5	1	6	4	3	2
3	2	4	1	6	5
4	5	1	6	2	3
6	3	2	5	4	1
1	4	3	2	5	6
2	6	5	3	1	4

Puzzle #165

1	6	2	4	5	3
3	4	5	1	6	2
5	2	6	3	4	1
4	1	3	5	2	6
6	5	1	2	3	4
2	3	4	6	1	5

Puzzle #166

1	5	2	6	3	4
4	6	3	5	2	1
5	3	6	1	4	2
2	1	4	3	5	6
3	2	1	4	6	5
6	4	5	2	1	3

Puzzle #167

2	6	4	1	3	5
5	1	3	2	4	6
1	5	6	3	2	4
4	3	2	6	5	1
6	2	5	4	1	3
3	4	1	5	6	2

Puzzle #168

3	6	1	5	4	2
4	5	2	1	6	3
5	1	4	2	3	6
2	3	6	4	5	1
6	2	5	3	1	4
1	4	3	6	2	5

Puzzle #169

5	3	6	2	4	1
2	1	4	3	5	6
4	5	2	1	6	3
3	6	1	5	2	4
6	2	3	4	1	5
1	4	5	6	3	2

Puzzle #170

6	4	1	3	5	2
3	5	2	6	1	4
5	2	3	1	4	6
1	6	4	2	3	5
4	1	6	5	2	3
2	3	5	4	6	1

Puzzle #171

6	4	2	1	3	5
5	3	1	2	6	4
2	5	3	6	4	1
1	6	4	3	5	2
3	1	5	4	2	6
4	2	6	5	1	3

Puzzle #172

5	3	2	1	6	4
6	4	1	3	5	2
3	2	6	4	1	5
4	1	5	6	2	3
1	5	3	2	4	6
2	6	4	5	3	1

Puzzle #173

6	2	3	1	4	5
1	5	4	3	6	2
5	3	6	2	1	4
2	4	1	6	5	3
3	6	5	4	2	1
4	1	2	5	3	6

Puzzle #174

1	6	4	5	3	2
5	3	2	1	4	6
2	5	6	3	1	4
3	4	1	6	2	5
6	2	3	4	5	1
4	1	5	2	6	3

Puzzle #175

5	2	4	1	3	6
6	1	3	4	2	5
4	3	1	5	6	2
2	6	5	3	4	1
3	5	6	2	1	4
1	4	2	6	5	3

Puzzle #176

5	6	2	4	3	1
4	1	3	2	6	5
1	3	4	6	5	2
2	5	6	3	1	4
3	2	1	5	4	6
6	4	5	1	2	3

Puzzle #177

5	1	2	3	4	6
4	6	3	5	1	2
3	4	1	2	6	5
6	2	5	1	3	4
2	3	6	4	5	1
1	5	4	6	2	3

Puzzle #178

3	4	1	2	5	6
2	5	6	4	1	3
6	3	4	5	2	1
1	2	5	3	6	4
5	1	3	6	4	2
4	6	2	1	3	5

Puzzle #179

2	4	5	3	6	1
6	1	3	2	4	5
1	3	2	4	5	6
4	5	6	1	2	3
5	2	1	6	3	4
3	6	4	5	1	2

Puzzle #180

3	2	1	6	5	4
4	6	5	1	3	2
1	3	2	4	6	5
6	5	4	3	2	1
5	1	3	2	4	6
2	4	6	5	1	3

Puzzle #181

6	1	3	4	5	2
4	5	2	6	1	3
2	3	5	1	6	4
1	4	6	3	2	5
3	2	1	5	4	6
5	6	4	2	3	1

Puzzle #182

3	2	6	4	1	5
1	4	5	6	3	2
4	6	2	3	5	1
5	1	3	2	4	6
2	5	4	1	6	3
6	3	1	5	2	4

Puzzle #183

5	6	4	2	1	3
2	1	3	4	5	6
4	5	1	6	3	2
3	2	6	1	4	5
6	4	5	3	2	1
1	3	2	5	6	4

Puzzle #184

5	6	2	3	4	1
1	4	3	2	6	5
2	1	6	4	5	3
4	3	5	1	2	6
6	2	1	5	3	4
3	5	4	6	1	2

Puzzle #185

2	5	3	6	1	4
1	6	4	2	3	5
4	1	6	5	2	3
3	2	5	1	4	6
6	3	1	4	5	2
5	4	2	3	6	1

Puzzle #186

4	5	3	6	2	1
1	6	2	3	4	5
3	1	4	2	5	6
6	2	5	1	3	4
5	3	1	4	6	2
2	4	6	5	1	3

Puzzle #187

3	4	1	6	2	5
2	5	6	4	1	3
4	2	3	1	5	6
1	6	5	3	4	2
5	3	4	2	6	1
6	1	2	5	3	4

Puzzle #188

5	4	1	3	2	6
6	2	3	4	5	1
2	3	6	5	1	4
1	5	4	2	6	3
3	6	2	1	4	5
4	1	5	6	3	2

Puzzle #189

5	6	4	2	3	1
1	2	3	5	4	6
6	1	2	3	5	4
4	3	5	1	6	2
3	4	1	6	2	5
2	5	6	4	1	3

Puzzle #190

1	4	2	3	6	5
6	5	3	4	1	2
3	6	5	1	2	4
4	2	1	5	3	6
2	3	4	6	5	1
5	1	6	2	4	3

Puzzle #191

5	1	2	3	6	4
3	6	4	1	5	2
1	4	5	6	2	3
6	2	3	5	4	1
2	5	1	4	3	6
4	3	6	2	1	5

Puzzle #192

1	3	2	5	4	6
5	4	6	1	3	2
3	6	4	2	1	5
2	5	1	3	6	4
4	1	5	6	2	3
6	2	3	4	5	1

Puzzle #193

3	4	5	1	6	2
2	1	6	3	5	4
5	6	2	4	3	1
4	3	1	6	2	5
1	5	3	2	4	6
6	2	4	5	1	3

Puzzle #194

2	1	3	6	4	5
6	4	5	1	2	3
1	2	4	5	3	6
3	5	6	4	1	2
4	6	2	3	5	1
5	3	1	2	6	4

Puzzle #195

2	1	4	3	6	5
5	6	3	4	2	1
1	3	2	6	5	4
4	5	6	2	1	3
6	4	5	1	3	2
3	2	1	5	4	6

Puzzle #196

4	3	5	2	6	1
6	1	2	5	3	4
1	6	4	3	2	5
2	5	3	4	1	6
3	4	6	1	5	2
5	2	1	6	4	3

Puzzle #197

5	3	4	6	1	2
2	6	1	5	4	3
3	1	5	2	6	4
6	4	2	3	5	1
1	5	3	4	2	6
4	2	6	1	3	5

Puzzle #198

4	5	2	3	1	6
6	3	1	4	2	5
3	2	6	5	4	1
1	4	5	6	3	2
2	6	4	1	5	3
5	1	3	2	6	4

Puzzle #199

2	1	5	4	6	3
6	4	3	2	1	5
3	5	2	1	4	6
1	6	4	5	3	2
5	3	1	6	2	4
4	2	6	3	5	1

Puzzle #200

2	1	4	5	6	3
3	6	5	4	2	1
6	4	3	1	5	2
5	2	1	3	4	6
1	5	6	2	3	4
4	3	2	6	1	5

Puzzle #201

2	3	4	5	6	1
1	5	6	3	2	4
6	2	5	1	4	3
4	1	3	2	5	6
3	6	2	4	1	5
5	4	1	6	3	2

Puzzle #202

6	2	5	3	1	4
1	4	3	5	2	6
3	1	4	2	6	5
2	5	6	4	3	1
4	3	1	6	5	2
5	6	2	1	4	3

Puzzle #203

6	4	1	2	3	5
3	5	2	6	4	1
2	1	6	4	5	3
5	3	4	1	6	2
1	6	5	3	2	4
4	2	3	5	1	6

Puzzle #204

4	6	1	3	2	5
5	3	2	1	4	6
2	1	4	5	6	3
3	5	6	4	1	2
1	2	5	6	3	4
6	4	3	2	5	1

Puzzle #205

1	6	4	5	2	3
5	3	2	6	4	1
3	2	5	1	6	4
4	1	6	2	3	5
2	5	3	4	1	6
6	4	1	3	5	2

Puzzle #206

3	6	5	4	2	1
1	4	2	3	5	6
5	2	3	1	6	4
6	1	4	5	3	2
2	3	1	6	4	5
4	5	6	2	1	3

Puzzle #207

1	4	2	6	3	5
6	3	5	1	2	4
4	6	1	2	5	3
5	2	3	4	1	6
2	5	4	3	6	1
3	1	6	5	4	2

Puzzle #208

2	3	4	6	5	1
5	6	1	4	2	3
4	2	3	1	6	5
1	5	6	3	4	2
6	1	5	2	3	4
3	4	2	5	1	6

Puzzle #209

4	3	1	6	5	2
5	2	6	3	1	4
6	4	5	2	3	1
2	1	3	5	4	6
1	5	2	4	6	3
3	6	4	1	2	5

Puzzle #210

3	5	2	4	6	1
4	1	6	2	5	3
6	4	5	1	3	2
1	2	3	6	4	5
5	6	1	3	2	4
2	3	4	5	1	6

Puzzle #211

2	6	4	3	5	1
1	3	5	2	6	4
5	2	1	6	4	3
6	4	3	5	1	2
4	5	2	1	3	6
3	1	6	4	2	5

Puzzle #212

3	6	1	5	2	4
2	4	5	6	3	1
4	3	2	1	5	6
5	1	6	2	4	3
1	2	4	3	6	5
6	5	3	4	1	2

Puzzle #213

3	6	2	5	4	1
1	5	4	2	6	3
2	4	5	3	1	6
6	1	3	4	2	5
5	2	1	6	3	4
4	3	6	1	5	2

Puzzle #214

4	5	6	3	2	1
1	3	2	4	5	6
2	6	4	1	3	5
3	1	5	2	6	4
5	2	1	6	4	3
6	4	3	5	1	2

Puzzle #215

1	4	3	2	6	5
6	2	5	1	3	4
4	1	2	3	5	6
3	5	6	4	2	1
5	3	4	6	1	2
2	6	1	5	4	3

Puzzle #216

6	4	5	2	3	1
1	2	3	5	6	4
2	1	6	4	5	3
3	5	4	1	2	6
5	6	1	3	4	2
4	3	2	6	1	5

Puzzle #217

4	5	2	1	3	6
3	1	6	4	5	2
5	3	1	2	6	4
2	6	4	3	1	5
6	2	3	5	4	1
1	4	5	6	2	3

Puzzle #218

6	2	4	1	3	5
5	3	1	2	4	6
3	5	2	4	6	1
4	1	6	3	5	2
1	6	3	5	2	4
2	4	5	6	1	3

Puzzle #219

4	2	5	6	1	3
6	3	1	4	2	5
2	6	4	3	5	1
1	5	3	2	4	6
3	1	2	5	6	4
5	4	6	1	3	2

Puzzle #220

2	4	3	1	6	5
1	5	6	4	2	3
4	2	5	6	3	1
6	3	1	2	5	4
5	1	2	3	4	6
3	6	4	5	1	2

Puzzle #221

5	4	2	1	3	6
1	3	6	4	5	2
6	2	5	3	1	4
4	1	3	2	6	5
2	5	1	6	4	3
3	6	4	5	2	1

Puzzle #222

6	4	1	2	3	5
2	5	3	1	4	6
1	3	4	6	5	2
5	6	2	3	1	4
4	1	6	5	2	3
3	2	5	4	6	1

Puzzle #223

2	6	1	4	3	5
4	3	5	6	2	1
5	2	4	1	6	3
6	1	3	2	5	4
1	5	2	3	4	6
3	4	6	5	1	2

Puzzle #224

4	2	1	6	3	5
5	6	3	2	4	1
2	1	6	3	5	4
3	4	5	1	2	6
6	3	4	5	1	2
1	5	2	4	6	3

Puzzle #225

2	6	4	1	3	5
5	3	1	2	4	6
6	5	3	4	2	1
4	1	2	6	5	3
1	4	5	3	6	2
3	2	6	5	1	4

Puzzle #226

4	6	3	5	1	2
5	1	2	3	6	4
3	5	4	6	2	1
6	2	1	4	5	3
1	3	6	2	4	5
2	4	5	1	3	6

Puzzle #227

2	6	1	3	4	5
4	3	5	1	6	2
3	4	6	2	5	1
1	5	2	4	3	6
6	1	3	5	2	4
5	2	4	6	1	3

Puzzle #228

2	5	1	3	6	4
3	6	4	5	2	1
5	4	6	1	3	2
1	3	2	6	4	5
4	1	3	2	5	6
6	2	5	4	1	3

Puzzle #229

2	6	1	4	3	5
5	3	4	2	6	1
1	2	5	3	4	6
6	4	3	5	1	2
3	5	6	1	2	4
4	1	2	6	5	3

Puzzle #230

1	3	6	2	5	4
5	4	2	1	6	3
2	1	5	4	3	6
4	6	3	5	2	1
6	2	1	3	4	5
3	5	4	6	1	2

Puzzle #231

6	3	1	4	5	2
5	4	2	6	1	3
1	6	3	2	4	5
4	2	5	3	6	1
3	1	6	5	2	4
2	5	4	1	3	6

Puzzle #232

4	3	2	5	1	6
6	5	1	2	4	3
1	4	6	3	5	2
5	2	3	1	6	4
3	6	5	4	2	1
2	1	4	6	3	5

Puzzle #233

2	1	4	3	5	6
6	3	5	1	4	2
5	2	3	6	1	4
4	6	1	2	3	5
1	4	6	5	2	3
3	5	2	4	6	1

Puzzle #234

5	2	4	1	3	6
1	3	6	4	2	5
3	5	2	6	1	4
4	6	1	2	5	3
2	4	3	5	6	1
6	1	5	3	4	2

Puzzle #235

2	4	3	1	6	5
1	6	5	4	2	3
6	5	4	2	3	1
3	1	2	5	4	6
5	2	6	3	1	4
4	3	1	6	5	2

Puzzle #236

4	1	5	2	3	6
3	2	6	5	4	1
1	5	3	4	6	2
6	4	2	3	1	5
5	3	1	6	2	4
2	6	4	1	5	3

Puzzle #237

6	2	5	3	4	1
1	4	3	2	6	5
2	5	6	4	1	3
4	3	1	5	2	6
5	1	2	6	3	4
3	6	4	1	5	2

Puzzle #238

5	3	2	4	1	6
4	1	6	3	2	5
3	6	5	1	4	2
1	2	4	5	6	3
2	4	3	6	5	1
6	5	1	2	3	4

Puzzle #239

5	2	6	4	1	3
1	3	4	2	5	6
6	4	1	5	3	2
3	5	2	1	6	4
4	1	3	6	2	5
2	6	5	3	4	1

Puzzle #240

3	4	1	6	5	2
6	5	2	1	3	4
2	1	5	3	4	6
4	3	6	5	2	1
1	2	3	4	6	5
5	6	4	2	1	3

Puzzle #241

4	3	1	2	5	6
6	2	5	3	4	1
3	1	4	6	2	5
2	5	6	4	1	3
1	6	2	5	3	4
5	4	3	1	6	2

Puzzle #242

6	2	3	1	4	5
4	1	5	2	6	3
3	4	1	6	5	2
5	6	2	4	3	1
2	5	6	3	1	4
1	3	4	5	2	6

Puzzle #243

4	3	5	1	6	2
1	6	2	4	3	5
2	5	3	6	4	1
6	4	1	2	5	3
3	2	4	5	1	6
5	1	6	3	2	4

Puzzle #244

5	4	1	2	3	6
3	6	2	4	5	1
1	3	5	6	4	2
4	2	6	5	1	3
2	1	4	3	6	5
6	5	3	1	2	4

Puzzle #245

2	4	3	1	5	6
1	5	6	4	2	3
6	2	4	3	1	5
3	1	5	2	6	4
5	3	2	6	4	1
4	6	1	5	3	2

Puzzle #246

2	1	3	6	4	5
4	6	5	2	3	1
6	4	2	5	1	3
3	5	1	4	6	2
5	3	6	1	2	4
1	2	4	3	5	6

Puzzle #247

4	1	2	5	6	3
5	3	6	2	1	4
1	4	3	6	2	5
2	6	5	4	3	1
3	2	4	1	5	6
6	5	1	3	4	2

Puzzle #248

2	4	6	3	5	1
3	1	5	2	4	6
1	5	2	6	3	4
4	6	3	5	1	2
6	3	4	1	2	5
5	2	1	4	6	3

Puzzle #249

3	1	2	5	4	6
5	4	6	2	1	3
4	5	1	6	3	2
6	2	3	1	5	4
1	6	4	3	2	5
2	3	5	4	6	1

Puzzle #250

3	2	5	4	1	6
4	6	1	5	2	3
1	3	6	2	4	5
2	5	4	6	3	1
5	4	3	1	6	2
6	1	2	3	5	4

Puzzle #251

6	5	4	3	1	2
3	2	1	4	5	6
1	3	2	6	4	5
4	6	5	2	3	1
2	1	3	5	6	4
5	4	6	1	2	3

Puzzle #252

3	4	2	6	1	5
5	1	6	4	3	2
6	5	1	3	2	4
4	2	3	5	6	1
1	6	5	2	4	3
2	3	4	1	5	6

Puzzle #253

6	5	3	2	4	1
4	2	1	3	5	6
3	4	5	6	1	2
2	1	6	5	3	4
5	6	4	1	2	3
1	3	2	4	6	5

Puzzle #254

2	3	6	4	1	5
4	1	5	2	3	6
5	2	1	6	4	3
6	4	3	5	2	1
1	6	4	3	5	2
3	5	2	1	6	4

Puzzle #255

3	6	1	4	5	2
5	4	2	3	6	1
1	2	4	6	3	5
6	5	3	2	1	4
4	1	6	5	2	3
2	3	5	1	4	6

Puzzle #256

3	2	1	6	4	5
4	5	6	2	1	3
2	1	5	3	6	4
6	3	4	1	5	2
1	4	2	5	3	6
5	6	3	4	2	1

Puzzle #257

5	6	3	2	1	4
4	1	2	5	6	3
1	5	4	6	3	2
2	3	6	1	4	5
3	2	1	4	5	6
6	4	5	3	2	1

Puzzle #258

2	1	4	3	5	6
3	6	5	1	2	4
5	4	2	6	3	1
6	3	1	2	4	5
1	5	3	4	6	2
4	2	6	5	1	3

Puzzle #259

3	5	1	4	6	2
6	2	4	5	3	1
2	4	6	3	1	5
1	3	5	2	4	6
4	1	2	6	5	3
5	6	3	1	2	4

Puzzle #260

4	3	5	6	2	1
6	2	1	3	5	4
2	6	4	5	1	3
1	5	3	4	6	2
3	1	6	2	4	5
5	4	2	1	3	6

Puzzle #261

6	3	1	5	2	4
4	5	2	6	3	1
3	6	5	1	4	2
2	1	4	3	5	6
5	2	6	4	1	3
1	4	3	2	6	5

Puzzle #262

6	4	3	5	1	2
5	2	1	4	3	6
1	3	6	2	4	5
2	5	4	1	6	3
4	6	5	3	2	1
3	1	2	6	5	4

Puzzle #263

2	1	4	3	6	5
6	5	3	2	4	1
1	3	5	4	2	6
4	6	2	5	1	3
5	2	1	6	3	4
3	4	6	1	5	2

Puzzle #264

4	2	6	1	5	3
3	5	1	2	4	6
2	4	3	6	1	5
6	1	5	3	2	4
5	3	2	4	6	1
1	6	4	5	3	2

Puzzle #265

5	2	4	3	1	6
3	6	1	2	4	5
1	4	6	5	3	2
2	5	3	4	6	1
4	1	2	6	5	3
6	3	5	1	2	4

Puzzle #266

1	4	3	6	2	5
6	5	2	1	3	4
3	1	5	4	6	2
4	2	6	3	5	1
2	3	4	5	1	6
5	6	1	2	4	3

Puzzle #267

1	6	3	2	5	4
2	5	4	3	1	6
3	1	6	4	2	5
5	4	2	6	3	1
4	3	1	5	6	2
6	2	5	1	4	3

Puzzle #268

6	3	1	2	5	4
2	5	4	3	1	6
1	4	2	5	6	3
5	6	3	1	4	2
3	1	6	4	2	5
4	2	5	6	3	1

Puzzle #269

4	3	2	5	6	1
1	5	6	3	2	4
6	1	5	2	4	3
3	2	4	6	1	5
5	6	1	4	3	2
2	4	3	1	5	6

Puzzle #270

2	6	1	5	4	3
3	5	4	1	2	6
6	1	2	3	5	4
4	3	5	6	1	2
5	2	3	4	6	1
1	4	6	2	3	5

Puzzle #271

3	1	2	5	4	6
6	4	5	1	2	3
1	5	6	2	3	4
4	2	3	6	1	5
5	3	1	4	6	2
2	6	4	3	5	1

Puzzle #272

6	2	4	5	1	3
5	3	1	6	2	4
2	5	6	3	4	1
4	1	3	2	6	5
1	6	5	4	3	2
3	4	2	1	5	6

Puzzle #273

5	4	1	3	2	6
6	3	2	1	5	4
3	1	5	6	4	2
2	6	4	5	1	3
1	2	3	4	6	5
4	5	6	2	3	1

Puzzle #274

3	2	4	6	1	5
5	1	6	3	2	4
4	6	3	1	5	2
2	5	1	4	6	3
6	4	2	5	3	1
1	3	5	2	4	6

Puzzle #275

4	6	5	3	1	2
1	3	2	6	4	5
6	1	3	2	5	4
5	2	4	1	3	6
3	5	6	4	2	1
2	4	1	5	6	3

Puzzle #276

1	4	3	5	6	2
6	5	2	4	1	3
2	3	1	6	5	4
5	6	4	3	2	1
4	2	6	1	3	5
3	1	5	2	4	6

Puzzle #277

5	6	2	1	4	3
4	3	1	2	5	6
6	4	3	5	1	2
2	1	5	3	6	4
3	5	6	4	2	1
1	2	4	6	3	5

Puzzle #278

2	4	1	5	6	3
3	5	6	2	4	1
5	3	4	6	1	2
6	1	2	3	5	4
4	6	3	1	2	5
1	2	5	4	3	6

Puzzle #279

5	1	3	4	6	2
6	4	2	3	1	5
2	6	5	1	3	4
4	3	1	2	5	6
3	2	6	5	4	1
1	5	4	6	2	3

Puzzle #280

4	6	5	2	1	3
3	2	1	4	6	5
2	3	6	5	4	1
5	1	4	3	2	6
6	4	3	1	5	2
1	5	2	6	3	4

Puzzle #281

5	2	6	3	4	1
4	3	1	5	6	2
6	5	3	1	2	4
2	1	4	6	5	3
1	4	5	2	3	6
3	6	2	4	1	5

Puzzle #282

2	4	3	5	1	6
6	5	1	2	3	4
3	6	5	4	2	1
1	2	4	6	5	3
4	3	2	1	6	5
5	1	6	3	4	2

Puzzle #283

2	6	1	4	5	3
3	5	4	6	2	1
5	2	3	1	4	6
4	1	6	5	3	2
1	4	2	3	6	5
6	3	5	2	1	4

Puzzle #284

1	2	5	4	3	6
4	3	6	5	1	2
5	6	3	1	2	4
2	1	4	6	5	3
3	4	1	2	6	5
6	5	2	3	4	1

Puzzle #285

6	4	3	1	2	5
2	1	5	4	3	6
5	6	2	3	1	4
1	3	4	6	5	2
3	5	6	2	4	1
4	2	1	5	6	3

Puzzle #286

5	1	6	3	2	4
4	3	2	6	5	1
6	4	5	1	3	2
3	2	1	4	6	5
1	5	3	2	4	6
2	6	4	5	1	3

Puzzle #287

1	3	4	6	2	5
6	5	2	4	3	1
3	1	5	2	4	6
4	2	6	5	1	3
5	4	1	3	6	2
2	6	3	1	5	4

Puzzle #288

5	2	1	3	6	4
4	6	3	2	5	1
1	5	6	4	3	2
2	3	4	6	1	5
6	1	2	5	4	3
3	4	5	1	2	6

Puzzle #289

4	3	1	2	6	5
2	5	6	3	4	1
1	4	3	6	5	2
5	6	2	1	3	4
6	1	5	4	2	3
3	2	4	5	1	6

Puzzle #290

3	2	4	6	1	5
6	1	5	2	4	3
2	6	1	5	3	4
4	5	3	1	2	6
5	4	2	3	6	1
1	3	6	4	5	2

Puzzle #291

1	5	6	4	3	2
2	4	3	1	5	6
5	3	2	6	4	1
4	6	1	3	2	5
6	2	4	5	1	3
3	1	5	2	6	4

Puzzle #292

6	2	3	5	4	1
4	1	5	2	6	3
3	5	6	1	2	4
2	4	1	3	5	6
5	3	4	6	1	2
1	6	2	4	3	5

Puzzle #293

2	1	3	6	5	4
6	5	4	1	2	3
1	4	2	5	3	6
5	3	6	4	1	2
3	6	5	2	4	1
4	2	1	3	6	5

Puzzle #294

4	6	3	1	2	5
2	1	5	4	3	6
6	4	1	2	5	3
3	5	2	6	1	4
1	3	6	5	4	2
5	2	4	3	6	1

Puzzle #295

5	2	6	3	4	1
4	3	1	6	5	2
2	4	5	1	3	6
1	6	3	4	2	5
3	1	2	5	6	4
6	5	4	2	1	3

Puzzle #296

5	1	6	2	3	4
4	2	3	1	5	6
2	3	1	6	4	5
6	4	5	3	1	2
3	6	4	5	2	1
1	5	2	4	6	3

Puzzle #297

1	4	3	2	6	5
5	6	2	4	3	1
2	5	6	3	1	4
4	3	1	6	5	2
6	2	5	1	4	3
3	1	4	5	2	6

Puzzle #298

2	5	4	1	6	3
3	6	1	4	5	2
5	1	3	2	4	6
4	2	6	5	3	1
6	4	2	3	1	5
1	3	5	6	2	4

Puzzle #299

5	4	1	3	2	6
3	6	2	1	4	5
1	2	4	5	6	3
6	5	3	2	1	4
4	1	5	6	3	2
2	3	6	4	5	1

Puzzle #300

2	5	1	6	3	4
6	3	4	5	1	2
5	1	6	4	2	3
4	2	3	1	5	6
1	6	2	3	4	5
3	4	5	2	6	1

CPSIA information can be obtained
at www.ICGtesting.com
Printed in the USA
BVHW011113140621
609525BV00003BA/236